AIR CAMPAIGN

IRAQ 2003

Precision wafare comes of age

MICHAEL NAPIER | ILLUSTRATED BY GARETH HECTOR

OSPREY PUBLISHING
Bloomsbury Publishing Plc
Kemp House, Chawley Park, Cumnor Hill, Oxford OX2 9PH, UK
Bloomsbury Publishing Ireland Limited,
29 Earlsfort Terrace, Dublin 2, D02 AY28, Ireland
1359 Broadway, 12th Floor, New York, NY 10018, USA
E-mail: info@ospreypublishing.com
www.ospreypublishing.com

OSPREY is a trademark of Osprey Publishing Ltd

First published in Great Britain in 2026

© Osprey Publishing Ltd, 2026

All rights reserved. No part of this publication may be: i) reproduced or transmitted in any form, electronic or mechanical, including photocopying, recording or by means of any information storage or retrieval system without prior permission in writing from the publishers; or ii) used or reproduced in any way for the training, development or operation of artificial intelligence (AI) technologies, including generative AI technologies. The rights holders expressly reserve this publication from the text and data mining exception as per Article 4(3) of the Digital Single Market Directive (EU) 2019/790.

A catalogue record for this book is available from the British Library.

ISBN: PB 9781472868053; eBook 9781472868022; ePDF 9781472868039; XML 9781472868046

26 27 28 29 30 10 9 8 7 6 5 4 3 2 1

Maps and Diagrams by www.bounford.com
3D BEVs by Paul Kime
Index by Mark Swift
Typeset by Lumina Datamatics Ltd
Printed by Repro India Ltd.

Title page caption: A B-52H Stratofortress from the 40th Expeditionary Bomb Squadron, with Joint Direct Attack Munitions (JDAM) loaded on the underwing pylons, heads toward Iraq for a close air support mission on 15 April 2003. Like the B-1B, the B-52 proved to be a surprisingly effective CAS platform. (NARA)

Osprey Publishing supports the Woodland Trust, the UK's leading woodland conservation charity.

To find out more about our authors and books visit www.ospreypublishing.com. Here you will find extracts, author interviews, details of forthcoming events and the option to sign up for our newsletter.

For product safety-related questions, contact productsafety@bloomsbury.com

Author's note

Timings of military operations are traditionally expressed in Greenwich Mean Time (GMT – also known as 'Zulu' Time), while US political decisions are generally expressed in Eastern Standard Time (EST). However, operations in and over Iraq took place in the diurnal frame of Baghdad Time, which is +3 hours from GMT and +8 hours from EST. Thus, an event which occurred for example in Iraq in the early morning there would be recorded in London as having occurred late at night on the previous day or in Washington as having occurred in the early evening of the previous day. For this reason, there are sometimes discrepancies between accounts which give differing dates for events. In this book, the Baghdad time/date is used, unless otherwise specified.

AIR CAMPAIGN

CONTENTS

INTRODUCTION	4
CHRONOLOGY	11
ATTACKER'S CAPABILITIES	13
DEFENDER'S CAPABILITIES	25
CAMPAIGN OBJECTIVES	32
THE CAMPAIGN	38
ANALYSIS	84
CONCLUSION	92
FURTHER READING	93
SELECTED GLOSSARY	94
INDEX	95

INTRODUCTION

Operation *Southern Watch* was always a Coalition effort: here an F/A-18 Hornet from the aircraft carrier USS *Carl Vinson* waits as two French Mirage 2000s refuel from a French C-135FR tanker aircraft on 23 April 1993. The French withdrew from the Coalition three years later. (NARA)

On 1 May 2003 aboard the aircraft carrier USS *Abraham Lincoln*, US President George W Bush declared that 'major combat operations in Iraq have ended. In the battle of Iraq, the United States and our allies have prevailed'. The campaign, known by Americans as Operation *Iraqi Freedom* (OIF) had started on the night of 19 March, after which, US-led Coalition forces fought an intensive and successful three-week military campaign to topple the Ba'ath regime and take control of Iraq. Thus, one might conclude that, with a definite start date and a definite end date, the Iraq War was a discrete and stand-alone conflict. However, that is not the full story, for in reality the Iraq War was merely a short campaign in a long conflict that stretched back to 1991 and had continued with varying intensity for the next 20 years. Indeed, hostilities continued in Iraq long after the war of 2003 had officially ended, and it was not until October 2011 that the next US President, Barack Obama, could announce that 'after nearly nine years, America's war in Iraq will be over'.

Nevertheless, it is certainly true that, as President Bush also said, 'Operation *Iraqi Freedom* was carried out with a combination of precision and speed and boldness the enemy did not expect, and the world had not seen before'. Indeed, the campaign was the first in which air power was fully integrated into conventional land warfare; a campaign in which precision-guided munitions released against targets which had been selected through an over-arching network of intelligence gathering ensured that air power was used with hitherto unseen efficiency and effectiveness. This book examines how air power was used during the Iraq War of 2003 – a textbook air campaign.

Background to the war

During the Gulf War of 1991, the Iraqi ground forces were driven from Kuwait by the US-led Coalition, but although the Iraqi regular army units suffered some appalling losses, the elite Republican Guard divisions extracted themselves from the battle area largely intact. This enabled Saddam Hussein to declare on 27 February 1991 that 'the harvest

President George W Bush announcing that 'major combat operations in Iraq have ended' from the flight deck of USS *Abraham Lincoln* on 1 May 2003. (US Navy)

in the mother of battles has succeeded' and thereby to present himself to other Arab nations as the honourable victor in an unequal struggle against Western imperialism. Thus emboldened, Saddam Hussein continued a policy of defiant confrontation against the USA and its allies for the next 12 years. Meanwhile, acting under the auspices of the United Nations (UN), a coalition comprising the USA, France and the UK established No-Fly Zones (NFZ) over Iraq. Two NFZ, one north of the 36th Parallel and the other south of the 32nd Parallel, were intended to prevent the Iraqi forces from using air power against dissident groups of Kurds in the north of the country and Shia Arabs in the south. Over the next ten years, Coalition aircraft and cruise missiles responded to Iraqi provocation with periodic airstrikes against Iraqi air defence facilities, notably in January 1993, September 1996, December 1998 and February 2001. The Southern NFZ was also extended up to the 33rd Parallel after the airstrikes in 1996. The US names for operations within the northerly and southerly NFZ were respectively Operation *Northern Watch* and Operation *Southern Watch* (OSW).

Meanwhile, the UN Special Commission (UNSCOM) for Iraq had been established under UN Security Council Resolution (UNSCR) 687 on 1 May 1991 to ensure Iraqi compliance with UNSCR directives banning Weapons of Mass Destruction (WMD). For the next six years, a team of UN weapons inspectors working on the ground in Iraq scoured the country, trying to ascertain whether or not Iraq had destroyed its stock of WMD. During this time, the Iraqi regime had perfected the art of 'cheat and retreat', whereby they would be uncooperative and obstructive up to and beyond any UN deadline but would then comply swiftly just before the US-led Coalition could take military action to enforce Iraqi compliance. Saddam Hussein thus gave the impression to the Arab world that he was confronting the USA as an equal and that he was only making concessions on his own terms. This policy also gave the Iraqis ample time to remove any incriminating evidence

OPPOSITE AIRFIELDS USED BY THE COALITION 2003

from their facilities before the UN inspectors had an opportunity to find it. The series of strikes in December 1998, known as Operation *Desert Fox*, came at the culmination of several years of Iraq taunting and interfering with the work of the UNSCOM weapons inspectors. Operation *Desert Fox* was a watershed for both sides. Afterwards the US Central Command (CENTCOM) began to update its OPLAN 1003, a contingency plan dating from eight years previously for an invasion of Iraq; meanwhile, for their part, the Iraqi air defences began a more confrontational stance against Coalition aircraft operating within the NFZs. From 1999, Coalition aircraft were frequently engaged by Surface-to-Air Missiles (SAM) and Anti-Aircraft Artillery (AAA). These incidents were met with retaliation by Coalition aircraft and there followed a period of what one RAF officer recalled as 'bombing various relatively cheap AAA pieces with a very expensive bomb, usually under SAM and AAA fire'. Nevertheless, despite this frustration, the Coalition continued to maintain air superiority within the NFZs and successfully limited the freedom of action of Iraqi forces below them. Operating in the NFZs also gave Coalition aircraft an unprecedented opportunity for reconnaissance, surveillance and intelligence gathering over much of Iraq.

A pair of F-15C Eagles aircraft from the USAF 1st Fighter Wing, on patrol in the No-Fly Zone (NFZ) over southern Iraq on 4 January 2002 in support of Operation *Southern Watch*. (NARA)

The terrorist attacks against the USA on 11 September 2001 hardened US policy against Iraq further, especially after President Bush declared a Global War on Terrorism. The strong suspicion that Iraq might use WMD in terror attacks against the USA or its allies led the President and his Secretary of Defense Donald Rumsfeld to conclude that an invasion of Iraq was the only way to neutralize that potential threat. Planning for a ground invasion of Iraq, with the aim both to neutralize WMD systems and to remove the Ba'ath regime, formally started in November 2001. At this time, the CENTCOM OPLAN 1003-98 was further refined, becoming OPLAN 1003V. This iteration of the plan envisaged a much lighter force to achieve its aim than had been used in 1991, by using surprise and advanced technology to ensure effectiveness on the battlefield. The plan was for a much shorter air campaign to shape the battlefield before ground forces were committed; by comparison, in the 1991 Gulf War the air campaign had preceded the ground phase by 38 days. To make this shorter air campaign possible, it was decided to use the aerial presence in the NFZs as an opportunity to carry out pre-emptive attacks to degrade the Iraqi air defence system in preparation for formal hostilities. This campaign, which was to be covert in as much as the Iraqis were not to be given any clues that it heralded full hostilities, was known as Operation *Southern Focus*.

The nature of 'retaliatory' raids by Coalition aircraft changed dramatically from 2002 with the commencement of Operation *Southern Focus*, and there followed a structured approach to dismantling the Iraqi air defence system. During 2002 there were 500 occasions when Iraqi air defence systems fired on Coalition aircraft, which resulted in some 90 retaliatory airstrikes against specifically selected elements of the air defence system. The daily tasking for Coalition aircraft into the NFZ was also adjusted to include surges of activity, so that the Iraqis became accustomed to random periods of increased activity which masked the deployment of yet more Coalition aircraft into the theatre. The pattern of randomized surges would also serve to hide the final preparations for the start of hostilities. As well as 'kinetic' operations involving the employment of weapons, reconnaissance and psychological warfare (PSYOP) missions were also flown in the NFZs.

During the four days of Operation *Desert Fox* in December 1998, numerous airstrikes were launched against military targets across Iraq. This F/A-18 Hornet is about to launch from USS *Enterprise* for a night-time strike on 17 December. (NARA)

Simultaneously with Operation *Southern Focus*, the USA pursued a course through the UN to obtain a clear legal framework for any military action. All of this political manoeuvring took place against the background of operations against al-Qaida and the Taliban in Afghanistan, after the invasion of that country by the US-led Coalition in 2001. Although the UN Security Council (UNSC) would not explicitly authorize military intervention in Iraq, as the Americans had hoped it would, it did pass Resolution 1441 in November 2002, warning Iraq of undefined 'serious consequences' if the country remained in breach of its obligations to the various UN monitoring agencies. At a further meeting of the UNSC on 6 February 2003, US Secretary of State Colin Powell presented evidence of Iraqi WMDs, but it still proved impossible for him to obtain a resolution expressly authorizing military action to intervene in Iraq. Nevertheless, the Bush administration, supported by Prime Minister Tony Blair in the UK, considered that there was sufficient legal justification for military intervention implicit in Resolution 1441.

Meanwhile, President Bush sought to build a 'Coalition of the Willing' who would support military intervention.

Here the lack of a more definitive authorization from the UN for a military solution was reflected in a reluctance, particularly amongst Arab countries, to support the USA. Even fellow NATO member Turkey denied the use of its territory and airspace for offensive operations against Iraq. Furthermore, although Western-leaning countries were sympathetic to the cause, only the UK committed large-scale ground forces to the Coalition; Australia did, however, commit Special Operations Forces (SOF). The UK and Australia also contributed combat aircraft to the Coalition. In early 2003 American, British and Australian forces began

This bomb damage assessment photograph of the Al Sahra Airfield, near Tikrit, Iraq, was used by Pentagon officials in a press briefing during *Desert Fox*, 18 December 1998. (NARA)

to assemble in the Gulf region in readiness for hostilities. Then on 18 March, with all his forces in place, President Bush issued a deadline to Saddam Hussein to leave Iraq within 48 hours or face a military invasion.

The role of air power

Slightly larger in area than California but slightly smaller than Sweden, Iraq is dominated by two great rivers, the Euphrates and Tigris, both of which rise in the Taurus mountains of eastern Turkey and flow southwards though Iraq to the Persian Gulf. Apart from the high Zagros mountain range which runs along the northern and north-eastern borders, most of the country is generally flat. The area to the south and west of the Euphrates is an arid desert, and most of the Iraqi population lives in the fertile area along and between the rivers. The populated areas also contain much of the industrial and military infrastructure, although a number of well-established airfields had been built in the desert during the 1970s and 80s. The arid climate in the desert region and the Mediterranean-like climate in the populated areas are well-suited to air operations: the weather factor is generally good, with predominantly clear skies and a short 'rainy season' in the mid-winter months. Thus, both the terrain and weather are ideal for flying during most of the year. A clear air mass makes photographic reconnaissance straightforward and also permits the use of laser guided weapons. However, both of these activities can be frustrated in the winter by the north-westerly *shamal* wind over Iraq, which is characterized by thick sandstorms that can last for days with windspeeds up to 40mph.

The unique speed and reach of air power had played an important part in the history of Iraq ever since the British had experimented with 'air control' of the country during the 1920s and 30s. This concept envisioned a small number of aircraft patrolling vast (and remote) areas over long distances far more quickly than even a large ground force could accomplish. If necessary, aircraft could also deliver decisive firepower to break up insurgent forces or put down revolts. This meant that substantially fewer ground troops were needed to maintain law and order, which in turn meant that the security budget could be reduced considerably. Thus, in theory at least, air power represented the most efficient way, both militarily and economically, to police Iraq and to protect its borders. Although air power was to play little part over Iraq in the 1940s through to the 1970s, and saw only limited use in the Iran–Iraq War of the 1980s, the Ba'athist regime had not forgotten the utility of air control for counter-insurgency operations: hence the establishment by the UN of the NFZs after the Gulf War to prevent Iraqi aircraft from being used against civil insurrections in the north and south of the country.

During OIF, air power offered a means of employing devastating firepower into the heart of Iraq to dismantle the command-and-control infrastructure and to destroy the will of the Iraqi army to fight. An array of airborne reconnaissance sensors could monitor activity across the country, feeding data back to the ground commanders giving them an unprecedented picture of the battlespace. Finally, in coordination with small SOF teams, aircraft could cover the vast area of the western desert to locate and neutralize elements of the Iraqi Tactical Ballistic Missile (TBM) capability. In all of these roles, the approach of Coalition air forces would be shaped both by their 12 years of operations in the Iraqi NFZs and by their recent operational experiences in Afghanistan.

CHRONOLOGY

2002
June The first Operation *Southern Focus* sorties are flown over southern Iraq.

2003
17 March President Bush issues an ultimatum to Saddam Hussein to leave Iraq within 48 hours.

19 March Late afternoon: Coalition SOF teams (including British and Australian troops) cross the border from Jordan into Iraq.

20 March 0230hrs: a 'Decapitation Raid' is mounted against Saddam Hussein by two F-117As.

Evening: US 1 Marine Division (1 MARDIV) moves into the Al Faw peninsula.

One CH-46E Sea Knight crashes close to the Kuwait-Iraqi border, killing the USMC crew of four and the eight British Royal Marine (RM) passengers.

21 March US Army 3rd Infantry Division (3rd Inf Div) crosses into Iraq.

2100hrs: the air campaign commences.

22 March 0430hrs: two RN Westland Sea King ASuC7 Airborne Surveillance and Control helicopters collide, killing six British and one US personnel.

1325hrs: an MQ-1 Predator destroys an Iraqi ZSU-34/4 self-propelled anti-aircraft gun near Al Amarah.

An F/A-18 Hornet performs first combat bomb drop by RAAF since Vietnam War.

The US Army 3rd Inf Div seizes Tallil airbase south of An Nasiriyah, as well as a bridge across the Euphrates River.

2030hrs: six MH-130 Combat Talons take off from Jordan on a mission to insert SOF teams into Sulaymaniyah and Bashur airfields in northern Iraq.

23 March 0248hrs: an RAF Tornado GR4 from Ali Al Salem airbase is shot down by a US Army Patriot SAM, killing the crew of two.

24 March 0115hrs: 31 AH-64 Apaches of the US Army 11th Aviation Regiment set out for a deep strike against Republican Guard units. One helicopter is shot down and its crew of two are captured.

1540hrs: A Patriot SAM radar locks onto a USAF F-16CJ which responds by firing an AGM-88 HARM at the radar.

25 March Ground operations in Iraq are brought to a halt by a *shamal* dust storm.

US Army 3rd Squadron 7th Cavalry are isolated on the enemy side of the Euphrates River at Abu Sukhayr, and call in a B-1B which drops 12 JDAMs, destroying ten T-72 tanks.

26 March Just before midnight the US Army 173rd Airborne Brigade conducts a large-scale parachute combat drop onto Bashur airfield.

27 March The *shamal* begins to abate. 3rd Inf Div attack isolates An Najaf.

2300hrs: a Spirit drops two precision-guided 4,500lb GBU-37 'bunker buster' bombs onto the Iraqi government communication tower on the eastern bank of the Tigris River in central Baghdad.

28 March A USAF A-10 misidentifies four British AFVs as Iraqi and strafes them, killing one trooper and wounding five others.

28 March A daily airlift of 12 C-17 Globemasters into Bashur airfield commences, eventually bringing another 1,200 troops into theatre.

2200hrs: the 11th Aviation Regiment carries out another deep strike Apache mission against the Medina Division of the Republican Guard.

31 March 3rd Inf Div seize the bridge over the Euphrates at Al Hindiyah and the 101st Airborne Div capture An Najaf airfield.

1 April The Republican Guard Baghdad Division opposite 1 MARDIV and the Republican Guard Medina Division facing 3rd Inf Div come under heavy air and land attack.

SOF troops of Task Force 20 capture the Haditha dam in the face of vigorous counterattacks by a strong Iraqi force.

0510hrs: a US Navy S-3B Viking is lost in a landing accident on USS *Constellation*; both pilots eject successfully.

1940hrs: a US Marine Corps AV-8B Harrier crashes into the Persian Gulf while recovering to USS *Nassau*; the pilot ejects.

2 April Just after midnight on 1 April, SOF teams mount a rescue mission to recover Private Jessica D Lynch, a US prisoner of war, from An Nasiriyah.

3rd Inf Div advance northwards and penetrate the Karbala Gap.

1 MARDIV crossed the Tigris River at Al Kut.

0150hrs: a US Navy F-14A Tomcat is lost in the early hours while supporting TF20. The crew of two eject safely.

1930hrs: a US Army MH-60L Black Hawk DAP crashes in the vicinity of Karbala, killing seven of the 11 personnel on board.

2330hrs: a US Army Patriot battery shoots down a US Navy F/A-18C Hornet from USS *Kitty Hawk* as it returns from a strike mission north of Karbala. The pilot is killed.

4 April Saddam International Airport on the western outskirts of Baghdad is captured by 3rd Inf Div.

0530hrs: two US aircraft drop LGBs on a house in Basra in an attempt to kill Gen Ali Hassan al-Majid, a cousin of Saddam Hussein, otherwise known as 'Chemical Ali'.

5 April A US Marine Corps AH-1W SuperCobra crashes killing the crew of two.

3rd Inf Div mounts a 'Thunder Run' high speed dash by armoured vehicles into central Baghdad.

6 April A mixed force of US SOF teams and Kurdish *peshmerga* militia battle with Iraqi forces at the Debecka (Dibaga) crossroads south of Erbil.

7 April 0330hrs: a USAF F-15E Strike Eagle flies into the ground during weapon delivery, killing both crew members.

3rd Inf Div mounts a second armoured 'Thunder Run' into central Baghdad.

1400hrs: a B-1B bombs a building in the Al Mansour district of Baghdad 47 minutes after intelligence sources identify Saddam Hussein at that location.

8 April 1015hrs: a USAF A-10 is shot down by a SAM during a CAS sortie near Baghdad (formerly Saddam) International airport; the pilot ejects safely.

C-17 Globemasters deliver M1A1 Abrams tanks and other vehicles into Bashur airfield.

USMC troops secure the airstrip at Salman Pak, establishing it as a base for helicopters.

Just after dark, a USAF MC-130H Combat Talon becomes the first Coalition aircraft to land at Baghdad International Airport.

9 April Organized Iraqi defences in Baghdad finally collapse as 3rd Inf Div and 1 MARDIV troops push into the city. However, Coalition troops still meet pockets of resistance.

10 April Clearing operations continue in Baghdad.

Task Force (TF) Tripoli advances north towards Tikrit, where the last remnants of organized resistance still hold out.

11 April TF Tripoli moves into Tikrit.

USMC AV-8B Harriers deploy to the repaired airfield at An Numaniyah.

1 May President Bush decrees 'mission completed' on the aircraft carrier USS *Abraham Lincoln*.

ATTACKER'S CAPABILITIES

Central Command

The United States Central Command (CENTCOM), commanded by US Army General Tommy R Franks, was responsible for US military operations in the Middle East and Southwest Asia. By extension, it also controlled all Coalition operations within its area of responsibility, which extended from the eastern borders of Pakistan across to the western borders of Egypt. The main CENTCOM headquarters was at MacDill Air Force Base in Tampa, Florida, but a forward headquarters was established at Al Udeid in Qatar in 2002. Following the invasion of Afghanistan in 2001, CENTCOM directed combat operations in that country, as well as controlling operations in the NFZ over Iraq. Then, in late 2002, CENTCOM was tasked with the preparations for an invasion of Iraq. Although many aircraft deployed to the Middle East specifically for OIF, many of those already in theatre were committed to operations over both Iraq and Afghanistan.

CENTCOM air power was commanded by the Combined Force Air Component Commander (CFACC), Lt Gen T Michael Moseley. In early 2003 it was one of the most powerful air forces ever assembled and was drawn primarily from five services: the US Air Force (USAF), US Navy (USN), US Marine Corps (USMC), British Royal Air Force (RAF) and the Royal Australian Air Force (RAAF). All of these forces were controlled and coordinated by US Central Command Air Forces (CENTAF) which was headquartered at Shaw AFB, South Carolina, and had a Combined Air Operations Center (CAOC) in theatre at Prince Sultan Airbase (PSAB) in Saudi Arabia. CENTAF had no units under permanent command, but instead personnel and aircraft were rotated into theatre for temporary deployments, typically lasting three months. Nevertheless, thanks to the long-term commitment to the NFZ, most of the personnel attached to CENTAF at any time already had extensive experience of operating over Iraq. In addition to air force and navy assets, the US Army operated attack helicopters within its command structure, and a smaller number of helicopters were operated by the British Royal Navy (RN) and the British Army.

The formidable F-15E Strike Eagle night/all-weather strike aircraft would play an important part over Iraq and Afghanistan in early 2003. This Strike Eagle, photographed over Iraq in 2004, is armed with AIM-120A Advanced Medium Range Air-to-Air Missiles, AIM-9M Sidewinder missiles, GBU-12 500-lb bombs, and is equipped with a AN/AAQ-28(V) Litening AT targeting pod. (NARA)

ATTACKER'S CAPABILITIES

Lt Gen T Michael Moseley, a former F-15 Eagle pilot, was the Combined Force Air Component Commander (CFACC) during the Iraq War. (USAF)

The tankers and combat aircraft participating in OSW had flown from PSAB, but although the Saudi government was content for defensive aircraft to operate from PSAB, it would not allow offensive operations in support of an invasion of Iraq to be mounted from its territory. Similarly, despite using Incirlik airbase for operations in the northern NFZ, CENTAF was denied the use of the airfields in Turkey for any attack on Iraq. As a result, CENTAF offensive air operations during the Iraq War would be conducted from a relatively large number of bases scattered across the region: Al Jaber and Ali Al Salem airbases, in Kuwait, Shaikh Isa airbase in Bahrain, Al Udeid airbase in Qatar, Seeb, Masirah and Thumrait airbases in Oman as well as Diego Garcia, some 3,000mi away in the Indian Ocean. In addition, the Muwaffaq Salti airbase at Azraq and King Faisal airbase at Al-Jafr, in Jordan would be available for counter-Tactical Ballistic Missile (TBM) operations over the western desert of Iraq.

USAF

The largest proportion of aircraft during Operation *Iraqi Freedom* was provided by the USAF, whose contribution covered the whole spectrum of capability, including tanker and transport aircraft, strategic reconnaissance assets, air defence fighters, close support aircraft, tactical strike aircraft and strategic bombers. The enormous task of transferring military personnel, equipment and supplies into the CENTAF area fell to the USAF and was undertaken by Lockheed C-5 Galaxy, C-130 Hercules and C-141 Starlifters, and Boeing C-17 Globemasters. In addition to pure transport duties, all of these aircraft were also capable of supporting airborne forces if necessary. However, even the resources of Air Mobility Command, the air transport arm of the USAF, could not manage such a large-scale deployment, so the Civil Reserve Air Fleet (CRAF) was activated. This organization utilized civilian airliners which were contracted from the main US airline companies in time of crisis, and its aircraft were used to transfer personnel from the USA to the Middle East for OIF.

The Combined Air Operations Center (CAOC) at Al Udeid airbase, Qatar, which became operational in March 2003. Operations over Iraq during the Iraq War were directed from a similar facility in Saudi Arabia. (USAF)

Arguably the most important aircraft in the CENTAF order of battle were the AAR tankers, without which few tactical aircraft would have the range to reach into Iraq. The tanker force, which would play a critical role in operations over Iraq, included 33 McDonnell Douglas KC-10 Extenders based at Al Dhafra and 149 Boeing KC-135R/T Stratotankers which were based across Saudi Arabia, Jordan, Romania, Bulgaria and Turkey.

The prime USAF air defence aircraft was the McDonnell Douglas F-15C Eagle, probably the best air superiority fighter of its day. Equipped with an AN/APG-63 pulse-doppler radar, the single-seat F-15C could be armed with up to eight AIM-120 Advanced Medium Range Air-To-Air Missiles (AMRAAM), or a mix of four AMRAAMs and four AIM-9L/M Sidewinder AAMs, as well as an internal M61A1 20mm six-barrel cannon. During OSW missions, its endurance was routinely increased by AAR. As defensive assets, some 42 F-15C were permitted by the Saudi authorities to continue to operate from PSAB during OIF. Boeing E-3C Sentry Airborne Warning And Control System (AWACS) aircraft were used initially to direct air defence fighters but during OIF they also fulfilled the airborne command and control centre role for offensive aircraft, allocating targets to the ground attack missions. During the conflict there were 15 E-3C Sentrys operating from PSAB.

Another variant of the F-15, the F-15E Strike Eagle, fulfilled the night/all-weather strike role and 48 of these aircraft were based at Al Udeid airbase in Qatar, covering tasks in both Iraq and Afghanistan. The two-seat F-15E was equipped with a multi-mode AN/APG-70 radar as well as the AN/APG-13 Low-Altitude Navigation and Targeting Infrared for Night (LANTIRN) system which comprised two pods containing a Terrain Following Radar (TFR) and Forward Looking Infrared (FLIR) sensors, and a laser target designator. This equipment enabled the F-15E to strike targets with great accuracy, day or night and in all weathers. The principal weapons used by the F-15E were the AGM-130 Air-to-Surface Missile (ASM) and

The most numerous USAF-operated type in the conflict was the F-16C. The F-16CJ variant, seen here landing at Prince Sultan airbase, Saudi Arabia in October 2000, fulfilled the critical Suppression of Enemy Air Defence (SEAD) role with the AGM-88 High-speed Anti-Radiation Missile (HARM). (NARA)

the 2,000lb GBU-24 and 4,000lb GBU-28 Laser Guided Bombs (LGB). Also based at Al Udeid were 12 Lockheed F-117A Nighthawk stealth fighters, which by virtue of their low radar cross section could penetrate Iraqi air defences undetected. The F-117A could carry two LGBs in its internal bomb bay, but, with no radar, it was dependent on clear skies to find its target through infrared sensors.

The most numerous USAF tactical aircraft type involved in OIF was the General Dynamics F-16. A capable ground-attack aircraft, the F-16 could carry two 2,000lb bombs or, crucially, in the case of the F-16CJ, the AGM-88 High-Speed Anti-Radiation Missile (HARM). The Block 50 F-16CJ was equipped with the HARM Avionics/Launcher Interface Computer (ALIC), giving it a fully autonomous Suppression of Enemy Air Defence (SEAD) capability. As well as its air-to-ground capability, the F-16 was an impressive air defence fighter. Some 131 F-16C and F-16CJ fighters were deployed across the three airbases at Al Udeid, Al Jaber and Azraq. Also based at Azraq was a squadron of 18 Fairchild A-10A Thunderbolt specialist CAS aircraft, with a further 42 A-10s based at Al Jaber in the east. Weapon loads for the A-10 included both free-fall bombs and LGBs, as well as the AGM-65 Maverick missile (both IR and TV guided) and the 30mm GAU-8 rotary cannon. The specialist night CAS role was carried out by eight Lockheed AC-130U Spooky gunships. These aircraft were heavily armed with 40mm and 105mm cannon as well as 25mm gatling guns, but their size and lack of manoeuvrability meant that they could only be employed where there was no air or SAM threat.

In addition to the smaller tactical aircraft, the introduction of the GPS-guided Joint Direct Attack Munition (JDAM) meant that strategic bomber types such as the Rockwell B-1B Lancer, the Northrop Grumman B-2 Spirit and the Boeing B-52 Stratofortress could be switched to fulfil tactical tasks. The JDAM weapon system comprised a programmable guidance module that could be fitted to a standard bomb: individual target coordinates could be programmed into each weapon, enabling the aircraft to engage a number of different

The advent of precision-guided munitions, such as the GBU-31 Joint Direct Attack Munitions (JDAM) enabled strategic bombers to take on tactical air support roles. This B-52H Stratofortress from the 40th Expeditionary Bomb Squadron at Diego Garcia is armed in readiness for a mission over Iraq on 10 April 2003. (NARA)

targets with great accuracy and precision regardless of the weather conditions. Each B-1B, 11 of which operated from Thumrait, could carry 24 JDAMs and was also equipped with a Moving Target Indicator (MTI) facility in its radar, enabling it to locate and track mobile vehicles. At Diego Garcia, there were 14 B-52H Stratofortresses, which could also be armed with the AGM-86C Conventional Air Launched Cruise Missiles (CALCM). A further 14 B-52s operated from RAF Fairford in the UK. Four B-2s operated out of their home base at Whiteman Air Force Base, 55mi south-east of Kansas City, flying 20hr sorties to their targets and staging on the homeward leg via Diego Garcia.

Taking advantage of the NFZs, the USAF flew strategic reconnaissance missions using the 15 Lockheed U-2S Dragon Ladys from Al Dhafra airbase in the UAE. Flying at 70,000ft, these aircraft gathered multi-spectral electro-optic, infrared, and synthetic aperture radar imagery, as well as long-range high-definition camera film. A similar mission was fulfilled by the single Northrop Grumman RQ-4 Global Hawk Unmanned Air Vehicle (UAV), which could fly 26hr missions over Iraq. From space, the Onyx satellites equipped with Synthetic Aperture Radar (SAR) also monitored surface activity across Iraq. Further locating and tracking of moving battlefield targets was achieved by the seven Boeing E-8C Joint Surveillance Target Attack Radar System (JSTARS) which acted both as battle management command and control centres and as airborne sensors providing real-time data to land commanders. Eight Boeing RC-135V/W Rivet Joint aircraft gathered signals intelligence and by employing two or more aircraft in different orbits, signals could be triangulated to locate their source accurately. There were also two more very specialized C-135 derivatives in theatre: an RC-135S Cobra Ball, which was able to detect and locate ballistic missile launches, and an NKC-135 Big Crow electronic warfare platform, which, amongst other roles, provided electronic jamming of various Iraqi communication and radar systems, as well as broadcasting for psychological operations (PSYOP). Prior to hostilities, a Lockheed EC-130J Commando Solo aircraft began broadcasting in Arabic warning civilians to stay away from military installations. Eventually there would be eight Commando Solos making PSYOP broadcasts into Iraq.

The USAF had largely divested itself of tactical reconnaissance platforms, but nine General Atomics RQ-1 Predator UAVs fulfilled this task and were able to pass on target information to ground controllers or directly to other tactical aircraft. They could also mark targets with a laser designator. The other seven Predators in theatre were the MQ-1 variant, which were armed with AGM-114 Hellfire missiles and could engage targets autonomously.

Special Operations were supported by dedicated USAF units flying specially modified aircraft. These included MC-130H Combat Talon II transports which could also act as AAR tankers for SOF helicopters such as the Sikorsky MH-53M Pave Low. Specializing in clandestine infiltrations, these aircraft were equipped for night operations using NVGs (night vision goggles) as well as a Terrain Following Radar system.

USN

By early 2003 there were three US aircraft carriers in the Persian Gulf: USS *Kitty Hawk* (CV-63), *Constellation* (CV-64) and *Abraham Lincoln* (CVN-72). Of these, the *Abraham Lincoln* had already been at sea for nine months, but the USS *Nimitz* was approaching Malaysia en-route to relieve her. In addition to the carriers in the Gulf, two more carriers, USS *Theodore Roosevelt* (CVN-71) and *Harry S Truman* (CVN-75) were sailing in the eastern Mediterranean Sea. Each of these ships had a Carrier Air Wing comprising around 100 aeroplanes. These included the Grumman F-14A/B/D Tomcat, which was originally designed as a fleet defence fighter, but was now used as a tactical strike fighter. The aircraft could be equipped with the LANTIRN pod for offensive support missions and could also carry

Intelligence Surveillance Target Acquisition And Reconnaissance (ISTAR) was vitally important during the Iraq War. Part of that role was performed by the U-2S Dragon Lady, seen here taking off for a mission over Iraq on 11 April 2003. (NARA)

the Tactical Air Reconnaissance Pod System (TARPS) for the photoreconnaissance role. The Tomcat benefitted from a relatively long range and some F-14s were deployed ashore to operate from Al Udeid from where they could easily reach into western Iraq. The Tomcat had been superseded as an air defence fighter by the McDonnell Douglas F/A-18C Hornet, which was a 'swing role' fighter equally capable in the strike role. As a strike fighter, the Hornet could be armed with LGBs, JDAM, AGM-88 HARM, AGM-84 Stand-off Land Attack Missile – Extended Range (SLAM-ER) and the AGM-154 Joint Stand-off Weapon (JSOW), as well as free-fall munitions. However, the Hornet was limited by its relatively short range. With 250 Hornets in theatre (including those operated by the USMC and the RAAF), it was the most numerous aircraft type deployed during the Iraq War. A replacement variant, the F/A-18E/F Super Hornet was new into service and was not yet cleared to release most of the air-to-ground weapons carried by the F/A-18C, but it did lend itself to being a tactical AAR tanker. Another type that was suitable as a secondary AAR tanker was the Lockheed S-3B Viking. The primary role of the Viking was in anti-submarine warfare and anti-surface vessel operations and the aircraft would be used in monitoring activity in the Gulf waters.

One of the most important aircraft in the USN inventory was the Grumman EA-6B Prowler electronic warfare aircraft. With the demise of the USAF specialist SEAD aircraft, the McDonnell Douglas F-4G Wild Weasel and General Dynamics EF-111A Raven, the EA-6B was the only tactical aircraft in the CENTAF order of battle that could locate as well as jam enemy SAM and AAA radars. It was equipped with AN/ALQ-99 Tactical Jamming System pods and could be armed with the AGM-88 HARM. EA-6B support was an integral and vital part of all Coalition strike packages. The complement of the carrier air wings also included the Grumman E-2C Hawkeye airborne command and control aircraft. The E-2C would supplement the work of the USAF E-3C Sentry in co-ordinating Coalition air power over the Gulf and the Al Faw peninsula.

Twenty-eight Lockheed P-3C Orion Maritime Patrol Aircraft (MPA) were deployed into the Gulf region. The aircraft was equipped with high-resolution infrared imagery, a long-range electro-optical video camera, and inverse synthetic aperture/synthetic aperture radar and, although its primary mission was maritime, it had been used to great effect in an overland surveillance role in Afghanistan. Before the outbreak of hostilities in Iraq, the Orions had been involved monitoring sea activity in the Gulf: tracking ships and boats to interdict illegal 'sanction busting' cargoes and to monitor mine-laying activity. They also provided real-time reconnaissance of Iraqi activity in and around the port of Umm Qasr and along the inland waterways in southern Iraq, as well as the dispositions of Iraqi troops and the locations of Silkworm anti-ship missile batteries. On the commencement of hostilities, the P-3Cs were used particularly by the US Marines, just as they had in Afghanistan, to provide real-time imagery of the ground immediately in front of the Marine positions.

In addition to combat aircraft, the USN also deployed ships and submarines armed with the BGM-109 Tomahawk Land Attack Missiles (TLAM), a cruise missile which could be launched from the Red Sea or the Persian Gulf against targets in central Iraq. The long range of the TLAM meant that it could be employed against strategic targets such as command bunkers and communications nodes within the formidable SAM defences around the Baghdad-Tikrit area, thus reducing the risk to manned aircraft. However, the featureless nature of the desert in Iraq meant that the accuracy of the Terrain Contour Matching (TERCOM) navigation system used by the missile was reduced. For this reason, manned aircraft would still be required to attack precision targets within the Super-MEZ. Over 800 TLAMs were fired during the Iraq War.

USMC

The USMC deployed the 1st Marine Expeditionary Force (1 MEF) which comprised the 1st Marine Division (1 MARDIV), the 3rd Marine Air Wing (3 MAW) and their support elements as well as the British 40 and 42 Commando Royal Marines. Temporary Task Forces (TF), notably TF Tarawa and TF Tripoli, were also constituted from 1 MARDIV according to the demands of the tactical situation. The main elements of USMC air component were

Flying from both Al Jaber airbase in Kuwait and the assault ships in the Persian Gulf, US Marine Corps AV-8B Harriers provided close air support to the ground forces of 1st Marine Expeditionary Force. (NARA)

split into three parts: 3 MAW based in Kuwait and the two Amphibious Task Forces (ATF) in the Persian Gulf. In addition, 18 KC-130 Hercules transport and AAR tankers were based at Shaikh Isa airbase in Bahrain and ten EA-6B Prowlers were deployed to PSAB. ATF West comprised USS *Boxer* (LHD-4) and *Bonhomme Richard* (LHD-6), while ATF East comprised USS *Kearsarge* (LHD-3) and *Bataan* (LHD-5). In all there were 54 McDonnell Douglas AV-8B Harriers, 22 Bell AH-1W SuperCobra attack helicopters, as well as 38 Sikorsky CH-53E Sea Stallion and 44 Boeing CH-46E Sea Knight transport helicopters afloat. At Ali Al Salem, 3 MAW had another 36 AH-1W, 18 UH-1N, 16 CH-53E and 24 CH-46E helicopters under its command. The SuperCobra gunships were armed with a 20mm gatling cannon and AGM-114 Hellfire missiles. Also in Kuwait, at Al Jaber, the 3 MAW fixed-wing aircraft comprised another 16 McDonnell Douglas AV-8B Harriers and 60 F/A-18C/D Hornets. The two-seat F/A-18D Hornets were used frequently in the Strike Coordination And Reconnaissance (SCAR) role as roving Airborne Forward Air Controllers (AFAC). Aircraft were used by the USMC much in the way that the US Army used artillery, and helicopters and fixed-wing aircraft were integrated in the fire and movement plans of the ground troops.

Lt Gen Moseley agreed to the USMC request that the USMC air component be primarily allocated for direct support of USMC ground units, but he nevertheless insisted that all missions were tasked through the CAOC in order to ensure proper coordination of all Coalition air effort. In addition, any USMC F/A-18 missions in excess of the immediate needs of the 1 MEF were to be released back to the CAOC for tasking elsewhere in the theatre of operations.

RAF

The British contribution to operations in the northern and southern NFZ had comprised four Sepecat Jaguar GR3 ground attack aircraft which carried out reconnaissance missions in the northern NFZ flying from Incirlik, six Panavia Tornado F3 interceptors flying from PSAB which carried out air defence missions in the southern NFZ, and eight Panavia Tornado GR4 ground attack aircraft which were based at Ali Al Salem and used for reconnaissance and airstrikes in the south of Iraq. The initial plan for the British element of OIF, codenamed Operation *Telic*, was to increase the number of Jaguars at Incirlik and supplement them with 18 Tornado GR4 plus a British Aerospace Nimrod R1 Elint aircraft and four Boeing E-3D Sentry AWACS. In addition, 12 British Aerospace Harrier GR7 comprising Harrier Force North would be based at Batman in Turkey and a further six Harriers of Harrier Force West would deploy to Azraq for counter-TBM missions. Meanwhile the southerly Tornado F3 and GR4 detachments would be reinforced to 12 aircraft each.

However, when the Turkish government vetoed operations from Turkey, these plans had to be revised. The Tornado GR4 detachment at Ali Al Salem was increased to 19 aircraft, and a further 12 Tornado GR4 were dispatched to Al Udeid; the Harriers that would have formed Harrier Force North in Turkey were sent instead to Al Jaber, becoming Harrier Force South. Harrier Force West was increased to nine aircraft and was joined by two English Electric Canberra PR9 photoreconnaissance aircraft, which like the U-2, was an aging but nevertheless extremely effective platform. Additionally, five Lockheed C-130K Hercules C1/3 transports and six Boeing Chinook HC2 helicopters were deployed to King Faisal airbase in Jordan, tasked with support of SOF in the western desert. At PSAB the RAF contingent now included 14 Tornado F3, seven VC-10 AAR tankers, plus the E-3D Sentrys and Nimrod R1. Further intelligence gathering was provided by four Nimrod MR2 MPAs supporting Coalition counter-TBM efforts in the western desert. Another

The RAF deep interdiction capability was provided by the Tornado GR4, operating from Ali Al Salem airbase in Kuwait and Al Udeid airbase in Qatar. This aircraft, armed with Enhanced Paveway II LGBs is seen on a combat sortie from Al Udeid during the Iraq War. (R Spencer)

four Nimrod MR2 were based at Seeb for more traditional maritime tasks in the Persian Gulf, and four TriStar AAR tankers were deployed to Muharraq, in Bahrain.

By 2003 the Tornado F3 had evolved into a formidable interceptor which was armed with AMRAAM and AIM-9 or the MBDA Advanced Short Range Air-to-Air Missile (ASRAAM). The AI 24 Foxhunter radar and Joint Tactical Information Distribution System (JTIDS) link gave the crew excellent tactical awareness. The Tornado GR4 was also well-suited to operations over Iraq, armed primarily with Enhanced Pave Way II (EPW II) 1,000lb and EPW III 2,000lb bombs which could be either laser- or, like JDAM, GPS-guided. The MBDA Storm Shadow air launched cruise missile, with a range of some 340mi, would also have its operational debut launched from the Tornado GR4 during the conflict. Tornados could also operate in the SEAD role employing the MBDA Air Launched Anti-Radiation Missile (ALARM). Typical armament for the Harrier GR7 included EPW II and III, as well as free-fall bombs and the AGM-65G2 Maverick missiles. Both Tornado and Harrier were equipped with the Ferranti-GEC Thermal Imaging Airborne Laser Designator (TIALD) targeting pod.

A major British contribution to CENTAF was the provision of the seven Vickers VC-10 and four Lockheed TriStar AAR tankers, which were based at PSAB and Bahrain respectively. As well as being compatible with RAF aircraft, these probe-and-drogue tankers could be used by USN, USMC and RAAF aircraft and they represented a much-needed supplement to the overall Coalition tanker fleet. Some 40 per cent of the fuel offload from RAF tankers would be transferred to USN and USMC aircraft.

RAAF

The Australian participation in the Iraq War was codenamed Operation *Falconer*. In February 2003, 14 F/A-18A Hornets from 75 Squadron RAAF deployed to Al Udeid, where they were initially tasked to fly air defence missions protecting Coalition AWACS and AAR tanker aircraft. These aircraft had undergone the Hornet Upgrade programme giving them similar capabilities to the USN F/A-18C variant. The RAAF Hornets were loaded with both air-to-air and air-to-ground weapons and early in the conflict they were switched to the offensive air support role, armed with GBU-12 500lb LGBs. The RAAF also deployed two AP-3C Orion MPAs to Al Minhad Airbase in the UAE, from where they flew maritime patrols over the Persian Gulf as well as missions supporting ground forces. Three RAAF C-130 Hercules transports also augmented the Coalition airlift.

US Army

The US Army V Corps, comprising the 3rd Infantry Division and the 82nd and 101st Airborne Divisions, formed the main part of the Coalition land force component. Organic air support for V Corps was provided by the Boeing AH-64D Long Bow Apache attack helicopters of the 11th Aviation Regiment, 3rd Infantry Division. Armed with a 30mm chain gun and up to 16 AGM-114 Hellfire missiles, the Apache was a remarkably capable aircraft. It also had an impressive night/all-weather capability thanks to the Target Acquisition and Designation Sights/Pilot Night Vision System (TADS/PNVS) in the nose and the AN/APG-78 Longbow millimetric fire control radar, mounted on top of the main rotor mast. Longbow enabled the Apache crew to track 128 targets simultaneously and engage up to 16 of them. The main role of the Apache was the close air support of V Corps, but the 11th Aviation Regiment had enjoyed great success during Operation *Desert Storm* in 1991 with deep interdiction strikes against Iraqi Republican Guard units. The regiment leadership was keen to relive their previous glory and there was an expectation that the unit would be used again for long-range strikes against the Republican Guard.

US SOF teams, which would play a critical role in counter-TBM operations, establishing forward landing grounds and liaising with Kurdish *peshmerga* guerillas, were supported by the

As part of Operation *Falconer*, the RAAF deployed 14 F/A-18 Hornets from 75 Sqn RAAF to Al Udeid airbase in Qatar. Early in the conflict the Australian Hornets switched from their original air-to-air tasking, to carry out offensive support missions. Operation *Falconer* forces also included two AP-3C Orion maritime patrol aircraft and three C-130 Hercules transports. (T van Haren)

160th Special Operations Aviation Regiment (SOAR). The regiment operated by McDonnell Douglas AH-6J Little Bird, Sikorsky MH-53 Pave Low, Boeing MH-47D/E Chinook and Sikorsky MH-60L Black Hawk Direct Action Penetrator (DAP) helicopters, all of which were armed and equipped for night operations, and most of which were also AAR capable. In turn, these aircraft worked closely with the MH-130E Combat Talons of the USAF. The US Army also held the 173rd Airborne Brigade in readiness at Aviano, Italy, to execute a combat parachute assault into northern Iraq. The paratroops would be delivered to their drop zone by USAF C-17 Globemasters.

Army air defence units were equipped with the Raytheon MIM-104 PAC-3 (Patriot Advanced Capability) Patriot SAM. Like the Apache force, the Patriot units had established a formidable reputation during Operation *Desert Storm* by successfully intercepting numerous Iraqi TBMs. Once again, there was a high expectation that the success would be repeated. Despite the reliance on Patriot to provide air defence across the whole of the region, there appears to have been little coordination between the Army air defence units and the Coalition air component.

British Army and Royal Navy

The RN deployed the aircraft carrier HMS *Ark Royal* and helicopter carrier HMS *Ocean* into the Persian Gulf in January 2003. Between them they carried Westland Sea King HC4 troop carriers and Sea King ASaC7 early warning helicopters. Six naval Westland Lynx anti-submarine/anti-surface helicopters were also deployed, as were a further 12 army Lynx AH7/9 and ten Gazelle AH1 helicopters of 3 Regiment Army Air Corps. All of these rotary wing types would be involved in supporting British Army and Royal Marine Commando units, mainly on the Al Faw peninsula area, as well as Coalition naval operations in the northern Persian Gulf.

A fundamental component of the ISTAR sensor array was the RC-135V/W Rivet Joint electronic surveillance aircraft. This Rivet Joint is taking off from Souda Bay, Crete, for a mission in support of Operation *Iraqi Freedom* in April 2003. (NARA)

Two TLAM-armed RN submarines, HMS *Turbulent* and *Splendid*, were also deployed to the region. They would contribute to the TLAM strikes during the conflict.

Training and combat readiness

The USAF, USN, USMC and RAF all had over a decade of experience of operating over Iraq since the Gulf War of 1991 and subsequently in the northern and southern NFZ, so they were very familiar both with the environment and with working together. Further joint combat experience had been gained over the Balkans during the 1990s and all four services frequently trained together, for example in Exercise *Red Flag* held in Nevada, making close co-operation between them very straightforward. Thus, the USAF, USN, USMC and RAF were all well trained, well equipped and combat experienced. The RAAF had not been involved in combat operations since the Vietnam War some 30 years previously, but a strong professional ethos and plenty of experience working with its US counterparts during exercises meant that the RAAF aircrew were also well motivated and highly capable operators who could fit seamlessly into the Coalition air component.

The units earmarked for counter-TBM operations were also given specific-to-role training from late 2002. Because this mission was very specialized, the units allocated to it carried out extensive joint training before they were deployed into theatre. The training culminated in a special iteration of Exercise *Red Flag* which was run at Nellis airbase in Nevada in January 2003 in order to validate the procedures and to allow all the elements to practice working together. Thus, by the time the conflict started, the counter-TBM forces were exceptionally well prepared for their mission.

The years of practical operational experience over Iraq and the Balkans had also brought improvements to the air tasking system. During the Gulf War the CAOC planning cycle typically took 72 hours to publish the Air Tasking Order (ATO) which allocated missions and targets to the individual units. By 2001 this had been reduced considerably, and further experience in Afghanistan combined with the full spectrum of Intelligence, Surveillance, Target Acquisition and Reconnaissance (ISTAR) platforms meant that the 'sensor to shooter' interval for Time Sensitive Targets (TST) might be as short as 20 minutes. This meant that Coalition air power could react almost immediately to developments on and around the battlefield, giving it a significant advantage over the Iraqi forces.

Perhaps the most crucial capability of the Coalition air component was the ability to strike targets extremely accurately regardless of conditions. During the Gulf War, eight per cent of the weapons dropped were Precision Guided Munitions (PGM) but by early 2003 the majority of weapons in the Coalition inventory were PGMs, either laser guided, or, significantly, satellite-GPS guided. During operations over the Balkans the limitations of LGBs in less-than-ideal weather conditions became very apparent. The advent of GPS guidance meant that, provided the target's coordinates were precisely known, weapons could be dropped accurately even if laser guidance was not possible. The PGM factor was also a 'force multiplier' in that fewer aircraft were needed to strike targets because of the improved accuracy of weapon delivery.

By the beginning of March 2003, Lt Gen Moseley commanded a Coalition air component of 1,800 aircraft of highly varied and specialized roles from a diversity of units. However, common training and 12 years of shared operational experience moulded the whole fleet into a single homogenous force which stood ready to strike Iraq.

DEFENDER'S CAPABILITIES

Iraqi armed forces

The Iraqi armed forces comprised the Iraqi Air Force (IQAF), the Navy, the Regular Army, the Republican Guard, various militias and irregular forces, as well as a number of security and intelligence agencies. With the exception perhaps of the militias and irregulars, these forces were well trained and well equipped and, at a tactical level, well led. However, their overall operational effectiveness was frustrated by the restrictions placed on them by Saddam Hussein. For Saddam was obsessed with preventing a coup against himself and he considered that the threat against him from within Iraq was far greater than any external threat from the USA. For this reason, all Iraqi military forces were placed under command of his trusted younger son Qusay Hussein, and all the higher-level commands within the services were filled with loyal members of his clan from the Tikrit area. It seems that Saddam believed that it was unlikely that the USA would actually take military action, but that if it did so, then US forces could be held at a distance from Baghdad until international pressure would inevitably force the US government to withdraw them, leaving him securely in power.

Iraqi ground forces were well defended by capable surface-to-air missile systems, such as the Soviet-supplied 2K12 (SA-6). These SA-6 Transporter Erector Launchers (TELs) were photographed at Baghdad International Airport in May 2003. (NARA)

The Iraqi Air Force (*al-Quwwat al-Jawwiyah al-Iraqiyyah* (IQAF))

The Iraqi Air Defence Command, headed by Lt Gen Yassin Mohammed Shaheen, was a branch of the IQAF. Despite the periodic attacks by Coalition aircraft in the previous decade, Iraq still had effective and capable air defences in 2001. It included an integrated communications network, radars, SAMs, AAA and fighter aircraft. The personnel who operated these systems were well trained and after ten years of operating under Coalition surveillance and the threat of attack by Coalition aircraft, they were skilful tacticians.

OPPOSITE IRAQI AIR DEFENCES

Iraqi President Saddam Hussein kept tight control over the Iraqi military forces, which prevented them from operating together efficiently. Saddam was more worried by the threat of a domestic coup than of foreign invasion. (Getty Images)

The running of most of the aspects of the Iraqi military forces was delegated to Saddam's trusted younger son Qusay. It seems likely that Qusay also commanded the Iraqi Tactical Ballistic Missile force. (AFP/Getty Images)

With its headquarters and an Air Defence Operations Center (ADOC) in Baghdad, the Command was sub-divided into five air defence sectors:

- Sector 1, with a Sector Operations Center (SOC) at Taji, in the northern conurbation of Baghdad. This sector covered the central swathe of the country, from the border with Saudi Arabia in the west to the Iranian border in the east.
- Sector 2, with a SOC at Al Walid airbase (also known as H-3) near the Jordanian border, covering the western desert area.
- Sector 3, with a SOC at Imam Ali airbase (also known as Tallil) near Nasiriyah, covering the south-eastern part of the country.
- Sector 4, with a SOC at Al Hurriya airbase near Kirkuk, covering the northern region.
- Baghdad Sector, an independent sector with its own SOC responsible for the defence of Baghdad itself.

The infrastructure of the integrated air defence system dated originally to the 1980s with the KARI system which was installed by the French company Thomson-CSF (the name is derived from the French for Iraq spelt backwards). This system linked each SOC to the ADOC and allowed radar displays to be viewed centrally, and remotely from the radar heads. The radars themselves were a mixture of Soviet-era systems including P-14 (Tall King), P-15 (Flat Face), P-18 (Spoon Rest) and P-35 (Bar Lock) early warning radars, as well as P-15M2 (Squat Eye) target acquisition and PRV-9 (Thin Skin) height finder radars. A Tall King antenna and a French-built Volex III surveillance radar which were based near Baghdad, at a safe distance from the NFZ, provided reliable early warning to the Baghdad ADOC. The ADOC and SOCs, in turn, controlled SAM and AAA batteries and, via Intercept Operations Centers (IOC) within each SOC, fighter aircraft. Coalition airstrikes both during the Gulf War and in the subsequent decade had undoubtedly destroyed large parts of the infrastructure of the air defence system, but much of the ground environment was still functional. Furthermore, during the late 1990s and early 2000s, Chinese contractors had upgraded the integrated communications suite with fibre-optic cables, which were buried for protection, thus providing completely secure communications on which Coalition Signals Intelligence (SIGINT) could not eavesdrop.

Like the radars, most of the SAM systems in use by the Iraqis were of Soviet origin, including SA-2 and SA-3 static systems and SA-6, SA-8 and Roland mobile systems. At the beginning of the Iraq War, the Iraqis possessed some 60 SAM batteries. The AAA guns, of which there were around 6,000, were predominantly Soviet-supplied 57mm S-60 and 100mm KS-19 pieces. Although the SA-2 and SA-3 systems were nominally static, in the ten years of challenging the NFZ, the Iraqi Air Defence Command had perfected the technique of rapidly moving and re-siting the SAM batteries every few days, so that the Coalition had difficulty keeping track of their positions. In the Baghdad area, the missiles were transported on modified commercial articulated lorries and periodically distributed around the 24 pre-prepared sites that ringed the capital. Each battery was permanently mobile, occupying one site for two or three days, before redeploying to another site. With more sites than batteries it was impossible to predict which sites would be active, and which would be empty. Meanwhile the interlocking Missile Engagement Zones (MEZ) of the SAM batteries maintained a virtually impenetrable screen around the Baghdad–Tikrit area, known by Coalition forces as the

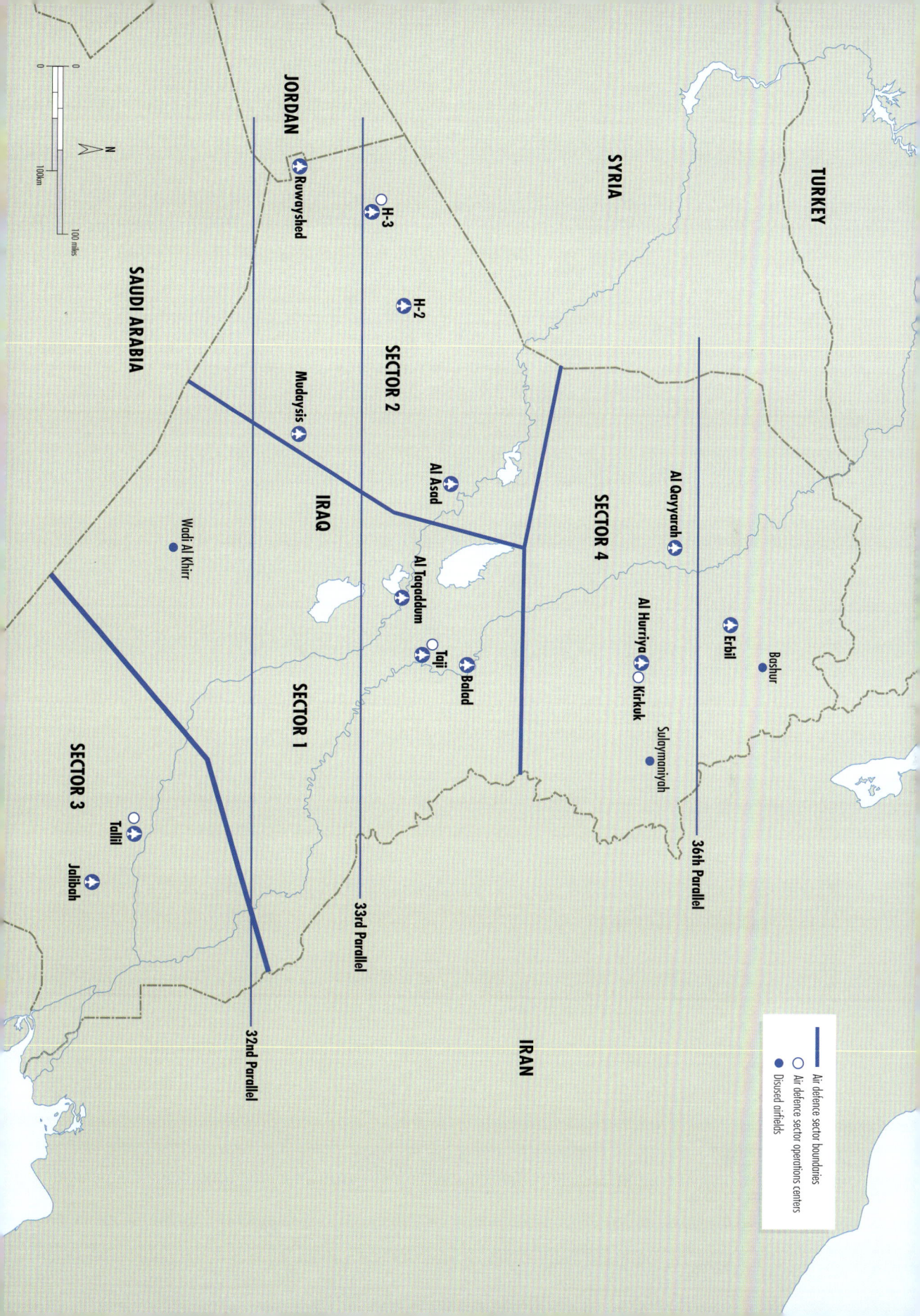

'Super-MEZ'. The main concentrations of SAMs and larger calibre AAA were in the Baghdad, Tikrit and Basra areas as well as at other important military or industrial facilities. The larger weapons systems were also augmented by smaller calibre guns such as the 37mm M-1939 and the ZSU-23/4 mobile system. Air defence radar operators were adept at using their equipment sequentially in coordination with other radars, so each radar transmitted for a short period before tracking was passed over to another radar, thus reducing their vulnerability to ARMs. Similarly, SAM operators aimed their missiles optically and fired them unguided, only switching on the target tracking radars in the last moments of the engagement to provide terminal guidance. In addition, some of the radar-guided SAMs were modified with infrared (IR) seeker heads. In summary, the ground-based Iraqi air defence was an effective and formidable force. It was an aggressive one, too: more than 100 SAM launches against Coalition aircraft were recorded between February and May 2001.

At its height during the Iran–Iraq War of the 1980s, the IQAF had been a large and powerful air force, with a modern inventory. However, much of that inventory had been destroyed or lost during the Gulf War of 1991, and subsequent arms embargos also resulted in many aircraft becoming unusable because of a lack of spare parts. As a result of these factors, the IQAF of 2003 was a much-reduced force with few of its MiG-21 (Fishbed), MiG-29 (Fulcrum), Su-22 (Fitter), Su-25 (Frogfoot) or Mirage F1EQ aircraft serviceable, but the IQAF still operated enough MiG-23 (Flogger) fighter-bombers and MiG-25 (Foxbat) fighters to remain a credible threat. The aircraft were mainly based at Al Taqaddum (to the west of Fallujah) and Al Asad (some 55mi north-west of Ramadi) but aircraft were also detached to other bases, including Erbil, Al Qayyarah, Balad and Al Hurriya (Kirkuk). During the 1970s, a number of large airfields had been built for the IQAF, featuring multiple runways as well as very robust Hardened Aircraft Shelters (HAS). These latter structures were known as 'Yugos' after the Yugoslavian companies that had built them. Despite the Coalition airstrikes during the Gulf War which destroyed many of the HAS and operating surfaces, the IQAF still flew from a number of these bases in 2003. These airfields were not covered by the NFZ so the IQAF could move aircraft covertly between

A MiG-25 Foxbat found buried in the sand at Al Taqaddum airbase, some 40mi west of Baghdad, soon after the end of hostilities. Despite still having a credible air-to-air capability with MiG-23 and MiG-25 fighters, the Iraqi Air Force took no part in the Iraq War of 2003. (NARA)

bases and the shelters on them. However, flying practice for Iraqi pilots was severely limited, with senior pilots flying some 60–120 hours per year, but junior pilots only flying as little as 20 hours in a year. All military flying was constrained by the NFZs, so training was also limited and tended to be unrealistic.

On the other hand, the MiG-25 squadron, which operated between six and 12 aircraft, was something of an elite unit in which was concentrated the most experienced IQAF pilots. It was these pilots who carried out the aggressive incursions into the NFZ. By late 2002 NFZ incursions were becoming a regular occurrence and on 24 September three MiG-25s violated the NFZ, flying deep into it and evading Coalition fighters. On 23 December, a MiG-25 shot down an RQ-1 Predator UAV within the southern NFZ.

Thus, in the run-up to the start of the Iraq War, the IQAF was still strong enough to present a threat to Coalition air operations, albeit probably at considerable cost to its own aircraft and pilots. However, Saddam decided not to commit his air power into the battle: instead, the pilots were ordered by the IQAF commander to go home and await further instructions. But no such instructions came, and some of the aircraft were buried in sand near their bases. It seems likely that Saddam was convinced of the survival of his regime and that he was attempting to preserve his air force so that it could fight another day.

The Republican Guard (*al-Haras al-Jamhuriy*)

A very professional and well-equipped organization, the Republican Guard represented the elite of the Iraqi armed services and was therefore a high priority target for the Coalition. There were eight Republican Guard Divisions divided between two Republican Guard Corps. In the late 1990s and early 2000s there was a sound plan for the defence of the country: an outer layer of defence manned by the regular army which would be supported by 1st Republican Guard Corps in the south and the 2nd Republican Guard Corps in the north. If the enemy broke through the regular army positions, the Republican Guard formations would conduct a fighting withdrawal to defensive lines which took full advantage of local topography and would then hold the invaders at some distance from Baghdad. The Republican guard also developed a concept of 'near and distant dispersal' in which equipment and personnel would be dispersed to make them less vulnerable to air attack. However, on 18 December 2002, Saddam Hussein unilaterally amended the defence plan for Iraq and changed its scope to the defence only of Baghdad. The Republican Guard divisions were to be deployed in a tight perimeter around, but remaining outside, the city and without any reference to local topography. Because Saddam was afraid of a coup against him, Republican Guard units were not permitted inside the city and nor were divisional commanders permitted to meet for coordinated planning. Thus, the Republican Guard found itself tied to tactically unsound positions and unable to manoeuvre, making its units easier targets for Coalition aircraft to attack. Nevertheless, this vulnerability was mitigated to some extent by the dispersal of personnel, equipment and weapons and by its inventory of powerful short-range anti-aircraft defences including SA-6, Roland and SA-8 radar-guided systems as well as SA-7 and SA-14 IR seeking Man Portable Air Defence Systems (MANPADS) and ZSU-23/4 AAA guns.

Other Iraqi land forces

In addition to the Republican Guard, the Special Republican Guard (*al-Ḥaras al-Iraq al-Jamhuriy al-Khas*) (SRG) comprising some 12,000 soldiers in five brigades formed a 'Praetorian Guard' for the personal defence of Saddam Hussein. Uniquely, the SRG was deployed in Baghdad, but was of little relevance to Coalition air power other than as a potential CAS target.

As well as SAMs, the air defences across Iraq included numerous Anti-Aircraft Artillery (AAA) batteries, comprising large guns up to 85mm, as well as smaller calibre weapons like this 23mm ZU-23-2 anti-aircraft gun mounted on a MT-LB armoured vehicle. (NARA)

In 2003 the majority of the 375,000 personnel in the Iraqi ground forces were in the regular Iraqi Army (*Al-jayshu al-Iraqi*), organized into 17 divisions divided into five corps. The Iraqi regular army did not enjoy the same prestige as the Republican Guard, which was reflected in inferior equipment; in addition, much of the fighting manpower was made up from conscripts rather than professional soldiers. However, the army was well trained and was led by a competent officer corps. Iraqi Army units were equipped with organic air defences such as SA-6, SA-8, ZSU-23/4 and MANPADS, but they did not achieve the same degree of operational competence as the Republican Guard. As outlined above, these troops would be the first line of defence and would therefore be early targets for Coalition air power. Under the defence plan devised by Saddam in December 2002, army units would eventually withdraw into built-up areas and entice Coalition forces to follow them into 'city bastions'. This would tie up the Coalition troops in urban warfare, thereby slowing their advance and ensuring that they were worn out before they reached the defensive line of the Republican Guards.

In 2003, Iraq was thought to possess between 12 and 25 Al-Husayn missiles, modified R-17 Elbrus (SCUD-B) TBM with an estimated range of 400mi, as well as a small number of Al-Samoud TBM which were based on the SA-2 SAM rocket, and also the shorter range Ababil-100 TBM. The exact command and control arrangements for the Iraqi TBM force remain unknown, but it seems likely that they were controlled by the Special Security Organization (SSO) (*Amn al-Khas*), another agency commanded by Qusay Hussein and operated by the Iraqi Army. Part of the premise on which George Bush built his case for invading Iraq was that Iraqi TBM could be armed with nuclear, biological or chemical warheads to cause mass destruction. The UN weapons inspectors had also noted spray equipment for distributing chemicals from helicopters. The Iraqi Army Aviation Command (*Qiadat Tayaran al-Jaysh al-Iraqi*) included Mil Mi-26 (Hind) and Aérospatiale SA-342 Gazelle attack helicopters, some of which were targeted during Operation *Desert Fox* because

Iraqi tactical ballistic missiles proved difficult to locate, as they were moved frequently between hidden locations, often by converted civilian lorries. Al-Samoud missiles were transported in trailers like this one, which was one of a number found in a suburban district of Baghdad in the last days of the conflict. (NARA)

of their potential chemical role. In 2003 the combat effectiveness of the Iraqi helicopter force was completely compromised by being transferred from the army command chain to be under the direct command of Saddam Hussein, who was possibly reserving them for chemical warfare operations.

In addition to the Republican Guards and the regular Iraqi Army, there were irregular forces, such as Saddam's Fedayeen (*Fida'iyyi Saddam*). This paramilitary organization had a strength of roughly 25,000 to 30,000, mainly made up of teenagers and young men. Chosen for their personal loyalty to Saddam, they were independent of the Iraqi military command. The Fedayeen was originally founded in 1994 by Uday Hussein as an internal security force, intended to counter criminal gangs and to suppress civil disturbances. They were lightly armed with automatic weapons and rocket propelled grenade (RPG) launchers, and recruits were given training in small-unit tactics, sabotage techniques and surveillance. In wartime, their task was to support the army firstly by carrying out suicide attacks on Coalition forces and secondly, once Coalition forces had been drawn into built up areas, to engage them with hit and run attacks. During the conflict the Fedayeen were notable for their fanaticism, probably due to the fact that a unit commander could expect the death penalty if his unit failed to achieve its task. Another irregular force, the Jerusalem Army (*Aysh al-Quds*), was formed in 2001, ostensibly to support the Palestinian uprising, but in practice it was just a loosely organized and poorly trained local militia based across Iraq. The Jerusalem Army played little part in the conflict. The challenge for Coalition aircraft giving close support to ground forces was firstly that irregular soldiers were indistinguishable from civilians and secondly that the tactics for urban CAS had not yet been perfected.

CAMPAIGN OBJECTIVES

OPLAN 1003V

Secretary of Defense Donald Rumsfeld, who began to consider an invasion of Iraq soon after the 11 September attacks by al-Qaida on New York and Washington. Rumsfeld had previously served as the Secretary of Defense in the late 1970s. (NARA)

A full-scale invasion of Iraq was first considered by Secretary of Defense Rumsfeld on 11 September 2001 in the aftermath of the al-Qaida attacks on New York and Washington. Two months later, after discussing the idea with President Bush, Rumsfeld instructed General Franks to look at a plan to invade Iraq. In turn, Franks decided to update CENTCOM OPLAN 1003-98 which had covered such a contingency but was now some three years out of date. The result was OPLAN 1003V, the aims of which were to remove the administration of Saddam Hussein and the Ba'ath Party, the elimination of Iraqi WMD and the dismantling of terrorist organizations that might be harboured by Iraq. The plan envisaged the focussed application of overwhelming force, defined by capability rather than numbers, delivering a swift 'knock-out blow' to the Iraqi military forces. After securing the oil fields, Coalition forces would advance quickly on Baghdad, bypassing the other cities en-route in order to capture the centre of government as soon as possible.

Detailed planning had started in December 2001 and British personnel were invited to join the CENTCOM planning team in July 2002, with Australian involvement following two months later. From the start there was some disagreement between land and air planners about how the operation should be initiated. The airmen, led by Lt Gen Moseley, favoured a high intensity air campaign lasting between one and two weeks to shape the battlefield before the commencement of land operations; on the other hand, Lt Gen David D McKiernan, the Combined Forces Land Component Commander (CFLCC), was keen to start the war with a land invasion. He argued firstly that air operations would destroy the element of surprise that would be necessary for the success of a 'lightning' campaign, and secondly that having lost that element, the high density of forces waiting in Kuwait for G-Day (the start of the ground offensive) would be vulnerable to attack by TBMs. Furthermore, he felt that it was vital to start counter-TBM operations with SOF troops at the earliest opportunity in order to reduce the chances of the Iraqis firing missiles at Israel. A compromise was reached in which a covert counter-TBM campaign by air and land SOF in the west of Iraq would be followed two days later by near-simultaneous starts of the air and land campaign against the main Iraqi forces.

Under the leadership of Gen Franks, all three services worked together harmoniously. Vice Adm Timothy J Keating, Commander naval component command of USCENTCOM (COMUSNAVCENT) later recalled that 'there was understanding, friendship, familiarity, and trust among all the services and special forces working for General Franks. He did, in my view, a remarkable job of engendering that friendship, camaraderie, and trust. In fact, he insisted on it'. Despite their differing perspectives on how the military operation should start, Moseley and McKiernan got on well together and their planning staffs worked together closely. Drawing on the lessons of Operation *Anaconda* in Afghanistan in March 2002, which had started badly because the army planners had not included the airmen in their arrangements, the inter-service coordination was further improved with the inclusion of Maj Gen Daniel P Leaf and his Air Component Coordination Element into the army headquarters in Kuwait. Leaf was able to ensure that both components fully understood what each expected of the other. Thus, planning for the air campaign over Iraq was completely inclusive not only of the air, ground and maritime elements, but also of Coalition partners, too.

A former artilleryman, US Army General Tommy R Franks commanded United States Central Command (CENTCOM) during OIF and oversaw the planning for the joint campaign in and over Iraq. (NARA)

The Coalition war plan included four main elements. Firstly, the invasion of southern Iraq by land forces which would follow the Euphrates River northwards towards Baghdad, approaching the city through the Karbala Gap from the south and west. This would be achieved by the US V Corps, comprising the 3rd Inf Div and elements of the 82nd and 101st Airborne Divisions, entering Iraq from Kuwait and would be complemented by the USMC 1 MEF. This latter force would carry out an amphibious assault on the Al Faw peninsula, then drive northwards along the Tigris River to approach Baghdad from the south-east. The landings on the Al Faw peninsula would achieve the second element – that of securing the Iraqi oilfields so that they could not be set alight as had happened in Kuwait during the Gulf War. Thirdly, US ground forces would invade northern Iraq from Turkey, following the Euphrates River southwards to complete the encirclement of Baghdad from the north. Unfortunately, it soon became apparent that Turkey would not allow offensive action to be launched from its territory, so in the final plan the opening of a limited northern front was to be achieved instead by an airborne assault. The fourth element of the plan was to locate and neutralize the Iraqi WMDs. During the Gulf War the SCUDs had been concealed in the western desert of Iraq from where they could strike at Israel, in the hope of dragging Israel into the conflict and thereby cause Arab nations to withdraw support for the Coalition. In 2003 the western desert would once again provide a vast area in which to hide the missiles, which might be used for the same purpose. The Coalition war plan depended on air power working closely with SOF to seek out and destroy the launching systems for Iraqi WMD before they could be launched against targets in Israel or Saudi Arabia.

Lt Gen David D McKiernan was the Combined Forces Land Component Commander (CFLCC) for OIF. With limited forces at his disposal, McKiernan was keen not to lose the advantage of surprise by running a long pre-invasion air campaign. (US Army)

In essence, the final iteration of OPLAN 1003V gave the air component five main objectives:

- The neutralization of the Iraqi command and control structure
- The suppression of Iraqi WMD including support of Coalition SOF
- The establishment of air supremacy over Iraq
- The support of Coalition land forces, including degrading the combat capability of Iraqi Army and Republican Guard forces before they could be engaged by Coalition land forces
- The support of Coalition maritime forces in the Persian Gulf

OPPOSITE KILL-BOX

This diagram illustrates the kill-box grid system, in which terrain is divided into alpha-numeric boxes, 30mins longitude by 30mins latitude. At the latitude of Iraq, these divisions equate to approximately 24nm east-west by 30nm north-south. Each 30min square can be sub-divided into nine 10min by 10min squares using a 'keypad' designation (so-called because it is the same layout as a phone keypad). The kill-box system, which was first used on a large scale in the Iraq War, greatly simplified the co-ordination between land and air forces.

An experienced naval aviator, V Adm Timothy J Keating, the Commander Naval Component Command at USCENTCOM (COMUSNAVCENT) was impressed with the co-operative way that the component commanders and their staffs worked together. (US Navy)

The critical concept in planning the air campaign was that of 'effects-based' targeting. In previous air campaigns, for example the Gulf War, some targets had been attacked simply because there was the capability to do so, and large target arrays had been 'carpet bombed' even though the required effect would have been achieved by an accurate strike on a single point within it. Using effects-based targeting, precise airstrikes would be made against targets which had been specifically chosen because of the effect that would be caused by their neutralization. Tasking would be focussed on achieving certain defined outcomes, rather than general destruction, and on ensuring that weapons were properly matched to their targets. The concept relied heavily on accurate intelligence, which could be gathered by the huge range of Coalition ISTAR platforms.

Before any of this could happen, though, a massive airlift was required to transport much of the equipment and supplies that would be needed for the campaign. Furthermore, as the ground campaign rolled forward at a swift pace, the ground forces would need to be kept resupplied with ammunition, fuel and rations. Most of the load would fall on USAF Air Mobility Command, but there was further support from British and Australian transport aircraft.

Without the preparatory air bombardment phase advocated by Moseley, the new plan relied upon Coalition air forces to take aggressive action within the NFZ well before formal combat operations started. They were also tasked with using their control over much of the Iraqi airspace as an opportunity for intelligence gathering. From mid-2002, air operations in the southern NFZ morphed into Operation *Southern Focus*, a series of airstrikes which were apparently launched in retaliation for Iraqi acts of aggression, but which were, in reality, part of a covert campaign to dismantle the Iraqi air defence system. Although Operation *Southern Focus* was not formally part of OIF, it was nevertheless a vital part of the overall plan. *Southern Focus* also meant that, at the commencement of OIF, the Coalition would already have established de facto air supremacy over most of Iraq, leaving a much reduced and degraded air defence system to be finished off in the first days of the conflict. While the F-15C, supported by the Tornado F3, would be expected to defeat the IQAF in the air, the prime weapon system against the surface threats would be the F-16CJ Wild Weasel and EA-6B Prowler armed with HARM.

Once formal hostilities began, attacks against the Iraqi command and control structure within the Baghdad–Tikrit 'Super-MEZ' would be carried out by F-117A Nighthawk and B-1B Spirit stealth aircraft. These aircraft would be able to penetrate the Super-MEZ without detection. Their attacks would be complemented by TLAM strikes by naval forces and CALCMs launched by B-52s. Anglo-French Storm Shadow missiles launched by RAF Tornado GR4s would also be used against hardened targets used by the Iraqi regime or

Kill-box grid system

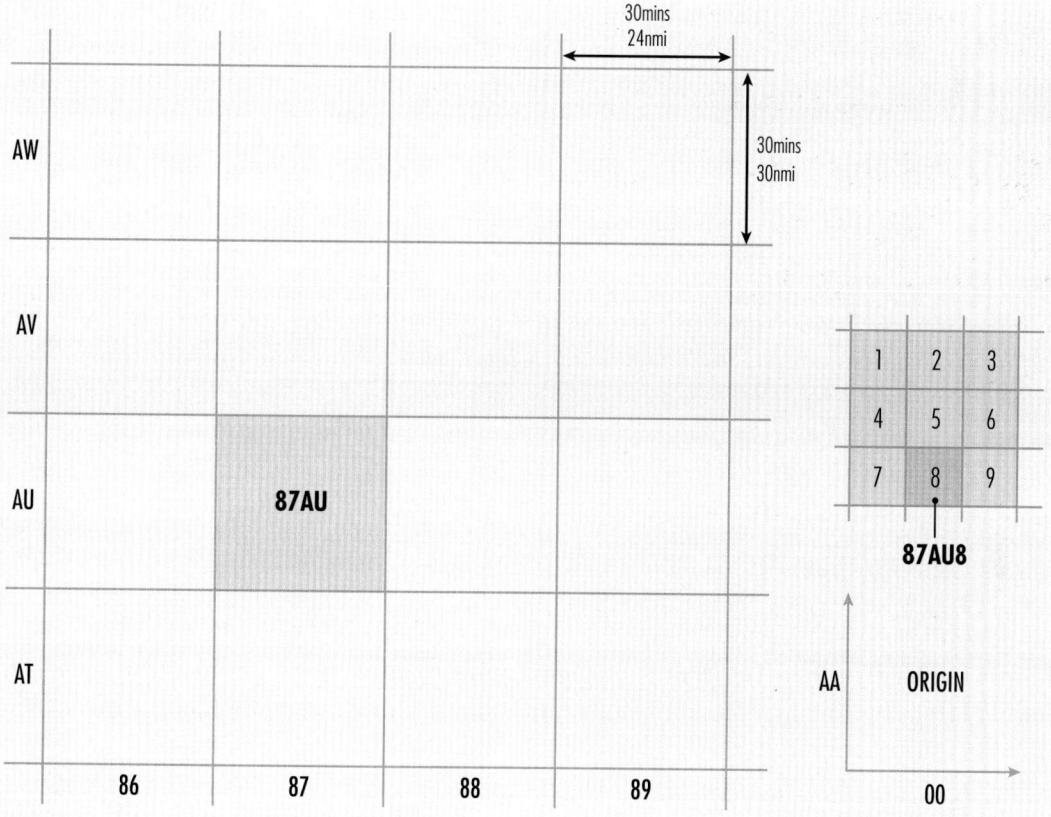

The main purpose of the kill-box system is to prevent fratricide, whilst increasing flexibility and minimising the amount of coordination required to fulfil support requirements. The kill-box concept has its origins in the 1980s, when the USAF sought a more efficient way of providing offensive air support, including both Close Air Support (CAS) and Air Interdiction (AI), to the land battle. Taking advantage of the accurate inertial or satellite guided navigation systems fitted in most modern aircraft, the kill-box could be defined entirely by grid co-ordinates, rather than by the visual features which had been needed by aircrew flying with less reliable navigation systems. Under the new system, the operational theatre would be divided into grid squares defining kill-boxes, which would be designated as 'open' when aircraft could attack any military target within the box without further clearance, or 'closed' when aircraft could only enter the box under positive control by a JFAC.

Kill-boxes were first used operationally during the 1991 Gulf War (Operation *Desert Storm*): during that campaign, those kill-boxes beyond the Fire Support Co-ordination Line (FSCL) were automatically 'open' unless specifically closed by the ground commander, while those on the friendly side of the FSCL were automatically 'closed' unless specifically opened by the ground commander. The system worked well and in the years after *Desert Storm*, each US Command developed its own methodology for defining and operating within kill-boxes. The kill-box system used in the 2003 Iraq War was the US CENTCOM system of 30min by 30min boxes, which equated on the ground to 24nm (east-west) by 30nm (north-south) boxes. Each box could be sub-divided into nine 'keypads' (so called because they were arranged in the same pattern as a digital keypad) each measuring 8 by 10nm. The Air Component Coordination Element (ACCE) Director, Major General Daniel P Leaf, reported that the 'kill-box/grid square method of deconflicting fires worked well and buy-in was complete at all levels by the end of offensive operations.'

Maj Gen Daniel P Leaf, who flew F-16 missions during the Kosovo War of 1999, commanded the Air Component Coordination Element at the army headquarters in Kuwait, ensuring that the air and ground forces worked together smoothly. (USAF)

its military forces. The success of all of these attacks relied heavily on satellite guidance and also accurate coordinates for the targets, which, in turn, depended on the ability of the array of reconnaissance sensors to locate them.

Close Air Support for Coalition land forces would be predominantly carried out by USAF A-10, F-16 and AC-130, and USMC AV-8 and F/A-18 as well as USN F/A-18 and RAF Harriers, while other ground-attack aircraft such as F-15E, F-16 and Tornado GR4, as well as B-1B and B-52 bombers would concentrate on the Republican Guard divisions and longer-range strategic targets. Because of the proximity of friendly forces and the risk of fratricide, all CAS missions were to be carried out under the control of a Forward Air Controller (FAC) and would be classified into three different types, depending on the tactical conditions and the relative locations of friendly and enemy forces. In Type 1 CAS the FAC must have visual contact with both target and the attacking aircraft. Type 2 CAS requires the FAC to be visual with the target or have accurate target data but does not need to see the attacking aircraft. Type 3 CAS, which is less restrictive and during which the FAC does not need to be visual with either target or attacking aircraft, is used when there is a need for clearance for multiple attacks within a single engagement and is subject to specific attack restrictions.

The integration of CAS missions into the ground campaign would be achieved slightly differently in the V Corps and 1 MEF areas of responsibility. In the case of V Corps, CAS missions would be allocated by the Air Support Operations Center (ASOC), and the missions would be tightly controlled by FACs between the Forward Line of Own Troops (FLOT) and the Fire Support Coordination Line (FSCL). In theory, supporting fire on the ground short of the FSCL was the responsibility of the artillery and thus directly controlled and coordinated by the Army tactical headquarters, but the ground beyond the FSCL was uncontrolled. The Army tended to rely on its artillery to provide fire support for infantry and armour and US Army doctrine was to push the FSCL as far forward as possible, sometimes as far as 85mi beyond the FLOT. On the other hand, the USMC lacked artillery and tended to rely on aircraft for firepower. CAS missions were allocated and controlled by the Direct Air Support Center (DASC), which sat at Divisional level, rather than the corps level of the ASOC. The USMC rarely pushed the FSCL further out than 14mi (the range of a 155mm howitzer) and also introduced a Battlefield Coordination Line (BCL) between the FLOT and FSCL, which allowed CAS missions some flexibility to operate without close control between the BCL and the FSCL. A new concept for interdiction and CAS tasking was also introduced, that of Kill-box Interdiction/CAS (KICAS). The kill-boxes were 30min longitude by 30min latitude (equating at the 30°– 40° latitude to 30nm by 24nm) boxes overlayed over the whole of Iraq. Each kill-box was identified by a unique coordinate system and could be further broken down into nine 'keypad' boxes each measuring ten by eight miles. Aircraft would be tasked into a kill-box and if the kill-box was beyond the FSCL the aircraft could engage any military activity detected within it; if the kill-box was short of the FSCL, then the aircraft would need clearance from a

FAC (either ground-based or airborne) before targets could be engaged. The KICAS was a very effective method of tasking aircraft into an operating area where the exact location of enemy forces was uncertain.

The dedicated force for Counter-TBM operations included an offensive support wing consisting of A-10, F-16 and Harriers supported by Canberra, Nimrod and RC-135S Cobra Ball reconnaissance aircraft. The campaign in the western desert would be run almost as a stand-alone operation, separated in space from the main thrust further to the east. The aircraft would be used both for searching for TBM launchers ('SCUD hunting') and providing CAS for the ground SOF teams that were also conducting searches for TBM launchers and their support echelons. These latter sorties would involve round-the-clock cover, so that the lightly armed SOF teams could be given almost instant support if needed.

Aircraft operating over Iraq would be flying from bases some considerable distance from their operating area; in addition, many of those aircraft were short range types or they needed to stay on station for extended periods. All of this could only be achieved by widespread and routine use of AAR. Thus, the most critical aspect of the whole air plan was the provision and efficient employment of the AAR tanker fleet. USAF KC-10s and KC-135s would be complemented by RAF VC-10s and TriStars. A complication was that USN, USMC and RAF strike aircraft used the 'probe-and-drogue' system for AAR, whereas the USAF used the 'boom-and-receptacle' system. Unless they were specifically modified, USAF tankers could not therefore refuel USN, USMC or RAF aircraft and in any case, RAF tankers could not refuel USAF aircraft. USN aircraft carriers could cover some of their own AAR needs by using the S-3 Viking and F/A-18E/F Super Hornet as tanker aircraft, but even so naval aircraft would still be largely reliant on USAF and RAF assets for refuelling. The inability to use Turkish airspace also complicated the planning, as the original plan had included tankers flying from Turkey to enable Coalition aircraft to strike targets in northern Iraq.

The lack of Turkish bases and overflight also complicated the plans for inserting SOF into northern Iraq to link up with Kurdish *peshmerga* guerillas. Infiltration flights would have to follow a much longer route via Jordan, adding to the risk involved as well as complicating mission planning. The carrier air wings in the Mediterranean Sea, which were to have operated over northern Iraq, also had to be re-routed.

However, despite these limitations, a viable plan for the air support of the ground invasion was in place by mid-March 2003. A massive air armada was in theatre and all the personnel involved in the forthcoming operation were well prepared for the tasks that they were to undertake. 'A-day' (the formal commencement of the air campaign), was set for 21 March, with 'G-day' following on the next morning.

Gulf War veteran AVM Glenn Torpy, a former Jaguar and Tornado GR1 pilot, who would later become the RAF Chief of the Air Staff, was the UK Air Component Commander during the conflict. (Crown Copyright/MoD)

Two EA-6B Prowler electronic warfare aircraft of the USN. The EA-6B played a vitally important role throughout the air campaign thanks to its extensive and unique suite of electronic warfare equipment, which included jamming transmitters capable of jamming Iraqi radar systems. (NARA)

THE CAMPAIGN

Operation Southern Focus

The first Operation *Southern Focus* sorties were flown in June 2002 and by September the airstrikes were becoming frequent. So, too, were Iraqi engagements with nearly 90 instances of SAM launches or AAA firings recorded in the second half of September alone. In June a pair of B-1Bs had destroyed a P-15 (Flat Face) SAM-3 acquisition radar near H-3 airfield, as well as a Selenia Pluto low-level surveillance radar sited close to both the Jordanian and Saudi borders. The airfield at H-3 was revisited on 5 September, when the SOC was bombed, taking down much of the air defence communications infrastructure for western Iraq. Overall, from June 2002 until the formal opening of hostilities in March 2003, Coalition aircraft dropped over 600 bombs during some 90 retaliatory airstrikes on 349 selected targets. One particularly challenging target set was the fibre-optic cable repeater stations, each of which was approximately the size of a manhole cover. Other targets included surveillance and acquisition radars, as well as SAM and AAA batteries. In addition, it was reckoned that by the eve of hostilities every SOC and IOC south of 33° North had been hit. By February 2003 Coalition aircraft were flying between 600 and 1,000 sorties into the NFZs on surge days.

One advantage of the freedom of movement throughout the Southern NFZ was that aircrews could familiarize themselves with the targets that they would be tasked against in the forthcoming air campaign. RAF Harrier pilots were even able to carry out a 'dress rehearsal' against their assigned wartime target, during a routine OSW mission. The NFZ airspace had also been divided into three 'lanes' running north–south, each of which was patrolled continuously by four or eight fighters, ready to counter any incursion into the NFZ by the IQAF.

By 17 March 2003, all the Coalition forces had deployed into the theatre and were ready for action. On that day, President Bush issued an ultimatum to Saddam Hussein that he 'and his sons must leave Iraq within 48 hours… Their refusal to do so will result in military conflict, commenced at a time of our choosing'. As the deadline approached on 19 March, aircraft carrying out routine OSW/Operation *Southern Focus* missions attacked a number of

A Canberra PR9 photoreconnaissance aircraft of 39 Sqn RAF. The aircraft operated from Jordan, flying missions over the western desert of Iraq as part of the counter-TBM campaign. (Crown Copyright/MoD)

communications and early warning sites near Mudaysis and Ruwayshed, as well as artillery positions on the Al Faw peninsula and a SAM battery near Basra. The air traffic control radar at Basra was also taken offline. At the same time, leaflets were dropped on Iraqi troops, instructing them how to surrender to Coalition forces.

Opening moves

Later that afternoon, Coalition SOF teams (including British and Australian troops) crossed the border from Jordan into Iraq, supported by AH-6 Little Bird and MH-60 DAP helicopters which neutralized the Iraqi observation posts along the border with Hellfire missiles. An RQ-1 Predator monitored their progress and transmitted live video to the CAOC. At 2000hrs, the British SOF contingent in TF 14 infiltrated from Arar using the six Chinook HC2 helicopters of 7 Sqn RAF. Overhead, aircraft were fully integrated into the SOF scheme of manoeuvre: a Nimrod MR2 orbiting just south of the Iraqi-Saudi

An F-117 Nighthawk from the 8th Expeditionary Fighter Sqn lands back at Al Udeid after completing the strike on the Dora Farms on 20 March 2003. This was one of the two F-117s that each struck an underground command bunker with two 2,000lb EGBU-27 bombs in the early hours. (US DoD)

EVENTS

1. Onyx satellite makes regular reconnaissance passes over the area of interest.

2. Photo reconnaissance overflights by U-2S and Canberra PR9 aircraft, searching for TBM launchers.

3. SOF teams advance into Iraq from Jordan 19 March.

4. A-10, F-16 and Harriers operating from Jordan establish Combat Air Patrols over SOF teams, ready to provide air support if required, as well as searching for TBM launchers.

5. F-15E, F-14D and Tornado GR4 operating from Qatar and Kuwait carry out armed reconnaissance flights over the western desert, searching for TBM launchers and providing air support to SOF teams.

6. Five MH-53M Pave Lows insert SOF teams to Wadi Al Khirr, 21 March, in preparation for three pairs of MC-130H Combat Talons and C-130K Hercules arriving the following night.

7. Chinooks operating from Arar insert SOF team TF 7 on 22 March.

8. Rangers seize H-1 in the early hours of 27 March.

9. SOF teams assault Iraqi positions at the Haditha dam, 31 March.

10. SOF teams operating against Iraqi forces around Al Qa'im, 5 April.

The Counter-TBM campaign in the western desert

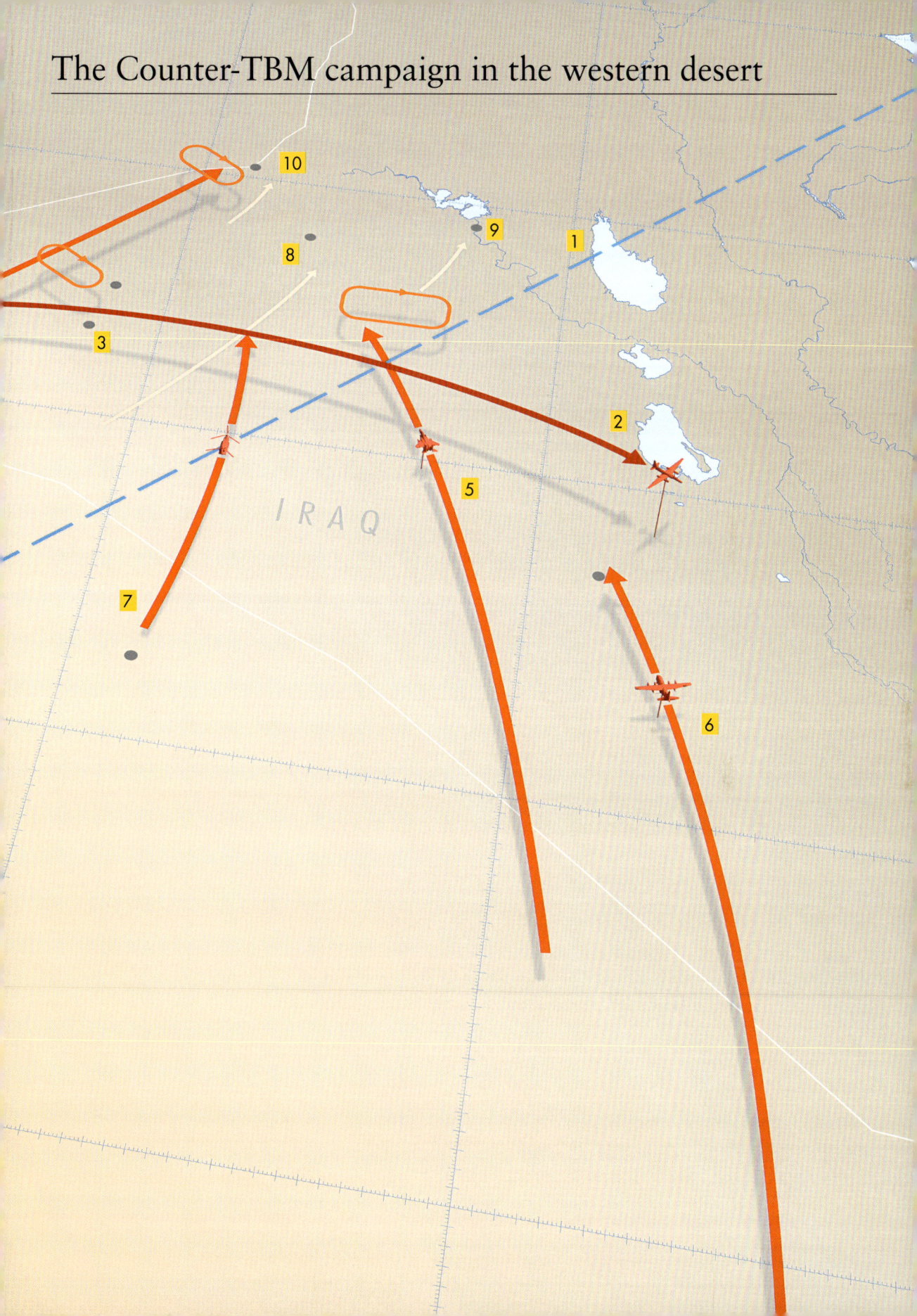

border used its MX-15 camera to alert the troops of any Iraqi forces moving towards them and relays of F-16s, A-10s and B-1Bs, as well as an AC-130 were on call to provide CAS wherever it was needed. At the same time, three pairs of RAF Harrier GR7s kept a continuous screen between the SOF teams and an Iraqi barracks which lay beyond the four-lane highway running between the Jordanian border and Rutbah. The Harriers were ready to intervene if Iraqi forces left the barracks and the pilots also used their TIALD pods to guide ground troops around inhabited areas in their path. By cycling through AAR tankers, the offensive support aircraft were able to maximize their time on task, with some pilots flying sortie durations of nearly nine hours.

According to the carefully arranged final plan for OIF, the air campaign was due to start at 2100hrs on the night of 21 March, with the ground offensive commencing at 0600hrs the following morning. However, during 19 March the Bush administration received credible intelligence from inside Iraq that Saddam Hussein and his two sons were due to meet that night at the Dora Farms in the southern suburbs of Baghdad. President Bush was thus presented with the opportunity for a precision strike to decapitate the Ba'ath leadership and possibly thereby achieve his aims without the further use of force. Such an airstrike could be carried out by F-117 stealth fighters armed with the newly acquired EGBU-27 GPS/Laser guided 2,000lb penetrator bomb. After deliberations in Washington, the airstrike was authorized at 0230hrs Baghdad time.

An hour later, two F-117s, flown by Lt Col David F Toomey and Maj Mark J Hoehn, took off from Al Udeid, each loaded with two EGBU-27s. Their target was a suspected underground bunker within the Dora Farms complex. The transit to Baghdad took two hours and the aircraft arrived over the city just as dawn was breaking at 0536hrs. The Stealth fighters were supported by two USMC EA-6Bs from PSAB and a further three EA-6Bs from USS *Constellation* which jammed Iraqi radars. In addition, a pair of F-16CJ Wild Weasels, led by Capt Paul Carlton were on station to supress any Iraqi SAM activity. Despite cloud which obscured the target area until just before weapons release, the two F-117 pilots delivered their weapons accurately into the Dora Farms and made their escape before they could be detected, just as a salvo of CALCMs and 40 TLAMs followed their own bomb strikes. The CALCMs had been launched by B-52s and the TLAMs were fired by US naval ships and submarines sailing in the Persian Gulf. The missiles were aimed at buildings in the Dora Farms complex and, in order not to compromise the intelligence sources, also at the headquarters of the Republican Guard and of the SSO in the centre of the city. Meanwhile, four F-15E Strike Eagles had bombed the IOC at H-3 airfield, using 4,000lb GBU-28 'bunker busting' LGBs, marking the last weapons to be employed on OSW: OIF had officially begun.

The Iraqi response to the attack on Baghdad was to launch a salvo of five SSM towards Kuwait. All of these missiles were intercepted by US Army Patriot PAC-3 SAMs. The launch of one Ababil-100 missile from just south of Basra was detected by the destroyer USS *Higgins*, which was able to geo-locate the launch site and send the coordinates to the CAOC. In turn, the information was passed to a pair of F-16s on patrol in the area, which then found and destroyed two launchers.

With the element of surprise now lost to the Coalition ground forces, it was decided to bring the schedule for the land campaign forward to the evening of 20 March; so rather than starting the morning after A-Day, the ground offensive now commenced before the air campaign. The master plan had been derailed before it had even started.

During 20 March the SOF teams in western Iraq were involved in a series of firefights with Iraqi forces and, despite poor weather over the area, A-10s, F-15Es and F-16s were called in to engage the Iraqi forces. RAF Harriers were also on call, although they were not used because they were not carrying GPS-guided weapons, and the weather conditions ruled out laser guidance. Instead, the Harriers carried out searches for SCUD launchers, using their TIALD pods as reconnaissance sensors. The Coalition aircraft maintained 24-hour coverage

Two F/A-18 Hornets (one from VFA-137 of the USN and the other from VMFA-323 of the USMC) prepare to launch from the flight deck of the aircraft carrier USS *Constellation* (CV 64) for a combat mission over Iraq on 20 March 2003. (NARA)

over the western desert, with each squadron or unit taking responsibility for four-hour blocks within that timeframe. That evening, in view of the meteorological conditions in the west, all-weather capable Tornado GR4s operating from Ali Al Salem airbase were also tasked to support the counter-TBM efforts. By the end of the day the SOF teams of Task Force (TF) 20 controlled most of the areas around the Iraqi airfields at H-2 and H-3. Despite the high intensity counter-TBM operations, there was little other air activity during daylight hours on 20 March.

As darkness fell that evening, the land campaign started with US Marines breaking out from Kuwait, and British Royal Marines landing on the Al Faw peninsula. The breakout commenced with a joint attack by F/A-18s, led by Lt Col Matthew Shihadeh USMC, dropping GBU-31 JDAMs onto the Iraqi observation post atop the Safwan Hill overlooking the Kuwaiti border. The Hornets were followed by 10 AH-1W attack helicopters. The plan was for the RM troops from 42 Commando to be landed by a 44-strong helicopter force comprising CH-46E Sea Knights and a CH-53E Super Stallion, supported by AH-1W SuperCobras, UH-1N Hueys, and an AC-130U Spooky gunship. However, the visibility was extremely poor due to dust and smoke from burning oilfields and one CH-46E in the first wave crashed close to the Kuwait-Iraqi border. The accident was unrelated to Iraqi action and was probably caused by the pilots becoming disorientated while flying on NVGs in poor weather. Sadly, the USMC crew of four and the eight RM passengers were killed. As a result of the crash, the mission commander Lt Col James R Braden USMC called for a weather abort. The Marines were flown into their objective later when conditions had improved. JDAM-armed F/A-18 Hornets, RAF Harrier GR7s and naval gunfire supported the operation. During the assault, a P-3C Orion detected an Iraqi PB-90 fast patrol boat sailing down the Khawr Abd Allah estuary towards the Coalition warships that were providing covering fire for the landings. The P-3C crew directed the AC-130U Spooky, flown by Capt Bill Holt and his crew known as 'the Lost Boys', towards the contact and the Iraqi boat was destroyed by the AC-130

A USAF F-15E Strike Eagle fighter over Iraq, carrying a variety of weapons including Paveway Laser Guided Bombs and AIM-120 advanced medium-range air-to-air missiles (AMRAAM). (NARA)

with gunfire from its 105mm cannon. Meanwhile a force of ten MH-53M Pave Low helicopters carried USN SEAL and British RM teams to capture the oil and gas rigs in the Persian Gulf.

Encountering light resistance on the ground, the Coalition troops quickly secured the Rumayla oil wells, including the strategically important pumping station at Az Zubayr, by 0300hrs. The Royal Marines also captured much of the port facilities at Umm Qasr, just to the north of Kuwait. RAF Harrier GR7s provided CAS to the Marines, destroying a number of Iraqi artillery batteries. At 0600hrs on 21 March, US 3rd Inf Div broke out from Kuwait and began to advance northwards. Since the US Army doctrine, unlike that of the US Marines, was to limit all air activity within the FSCL, the 3rd Inf Div advance was primarily supported by artillery and organic AH-64D Apache attack helicopters, although fixed-wing assets including RAF Harrier GR7s were also tasked to support the army. The first combat firing of an AGM-65G2 Maverick missile from a Harrier GR7 took place that day when Flt Lt Mike F Rutland engaged a mobile SAM launcher. Later, another formation of Harriers hit column of six Armoured Personnel Carriers (APCs) near Tallil with Mavericks. During the day, 3rd Inf Div made good progress and had penetrated 100mi into Iraq by the close of the first evening.

The Coalition air campaign commenced, as planned, at 2100hrs on 21 March. However, the Air Tasking Order had to be substantially revised to reflect the fact that many of the planned targets had already been overrun by Coalition ground forces or were within the FSCL. Nevertheless some 1,500 sorties, comprising 700 strike sorties and 800 support sorties, were flown on the first night of the air offensive and 100 CALCMs were launched by B-52s, some of which had flown from RAF Fairford in the UK. A further 500 TLAMs were launched by Coalition naval forces. The cruise missiles were fired against strategic targets in Baghdad, Kirkuk, Mosul and Tikrit. Simultaneous strikes by B-2 Spirits (which had flown all the way from their home base at Whiteman airbase in Missouri) and F-117 Nighthawks cratered the runways of the eight Iraqi airfields that were known to be operational, effectively closing them down. F-117 stealth fighters also struck five strategic targets in Baghdad, once again using the EGBU-27 penetrator bomb. Missions in the Super-MEZ were supported by numerous SEAD missions which were flown through the night by F-16CJ and F/A-18C, firing HARM in the Pre-Emptive Target (PET) mode and by F-15E strike aircraft, which bombed air defence installations. Ten radar-jamming EA-6B

An AH-1W SuperCobra attack helicopter of the USMC is refuelled by RAF groundcrew in Kuwait on 23 March 2003. The SuperCobra provided the first line of close air support for the US Marines. (Crown Copyright/MoD)

Prowlers constituted a vital part of the SEAD missions; additionally, two expendable Ryan BQM-34 Firebee drones fitted with chaff dispensers flew over Baghdad acting both to lay a chaff corridor and as expendable decoys. Although western media had predicted that the first day of the air campaign would be marked by 'shock and awe', little was actually seen of the attacks by the media, largely because they were carried out with great precision, so the results, either underground or within walled complexes were not visible to the casual observer. Furthermore, the civil infrastructure facilities, such as the electrical power grid, which might have made spectacular targets were not attacked in order not to alienate the Iraqi civilian population.

Six Tornado GR4s from Al Udeid targeted the runways and taxiways at Qayyarah West airfield. The night also saw the operational debut by the RAF of the Storm Shadow stand-off missile. A pair of Tornado GR4s, led by Sqn Ldr Andrew M Myers and Wg Cdr David Robertson and each loaded with two missiles, took off from Ali Al Salem and flew to a launch point to the west of Baghdad. Both aircraft were fired on by SAMs on their ingress, and the Number 2 aircraft, flown by Sqn Ldr David J Knowles and Flt Lt Andrew D Turk, was forced to jettison its external fuel tanks during the evasive manoeuvring. However, the two Tornados reached the launch point, from which they fired the Storm Shadows against the air defence sector headquarters, IOC and radar facility at Kirkuk. The aircraft which had jettisoned its fuel tanks was now running short of fuel and with no tankers available for support, the crew diverted to Arar airbase. At almost the same moment as the first salvo of Storm Shadows was launched towards Kirkuk, another pair of Tornado GR4s, led by Flt Lts Robert J Chevli and Andrew J Reardon, each fired two Storm Shadows at the air defence headquarters and IOC at Taji, just north of Baghdad. Then, as dawn broke on 22 March, four Tornado GR4s from the Al Udeid wing attacked a Republican Guard barracks at Saribadi with LGBs. Earlier, Tornado GR4s from Ali Al Salem had fired 17 ALARM II anti-radiation missiles into the Baghdad area to support US airstrikes.

Coinciding with the initial bombardment on 21 March, a force of five MH-53M Pave Lows infiltrated Iraq from Arar airbase in Saudi Arabia. They were carrying SOF troops to capture the derelict Iraqi airfield at Wadi Al Khirr, which had been abandoned 12 years previously at the end of the Gulf War. Reconnaissance previously carried out by RAF Tornados had confirmed that the runway at Wadi Al Khirr, though covered with debris, was probably still

OPPOSITE COALITION GROUND CAMPAIGN: 20–28 MARCH 2003

useable. The ingress by the SOF was not without its excitement, as the helicopters found themselves unexpectedly being overflown by TLAMs aimed at Baghdad, as they refuelled from a pair of MC-130P Combat Shadow AAR tankers. The helicopters touched down successfully at Wadi Al Khirr and their SOF teams busied themselves preparing the runway for use by MH-130H Combat Talons the following night.

Counter-TBM continued in the western desert and Coalition aircraft provided CAS for SOF teams as they scoured the area searching for TBM launchers. In particular, F-16s and RAF Harrier GR7s carried out a coordinated attack on the water treatment plant at Al Qa'im, which, according to intelligence sources, had recently been modified to incorporate prepared areas for firing SCUD missiles towards Israel. SOF teams also attempted to capture the township at Al Qa'im but met with stiff resistance from the Iraqi garrison. Once again Coalition aircraft were able to assist the efforts of the SOF teams with additional firepower. Al Qa'im was of particular strategic interest with regard to WMD since it had been the centre for uranium enrichment for the Iraqi nuclear weapons programme during the 1980s.

During the air assault the air defence lanes in the south of Iraq were patrolled by F-15C Eagles and Tornado F3s, flying six-to-seven-hour sorties. Radar coverage and control in the west was provided by RAF E-3D Sentry AWACS, while that in the east was by USAF E-3C AWACS, sometimes supplemented in the far eastern sector by USN E-2 Hawkeyes. The Coalition fighters were ready to engage any aircraft which took off from IQAF bases, but in the event the IQAF was notable by its complete absence. One Tornado F3 did intercept four unidentified aircraft flying fast and low over the desert, but as the crew got within visual range, they realized that these were TLAMs which had been launched by Coalition

An F-16CJ from the 555th Fighter Squadron over the Iraqi countryside, shortly after the conflict. Equipped with the HARM Avionics/Launcher Interface Computer (ALIC), the F-16CJ could operate in the SEAD role. (NARA)

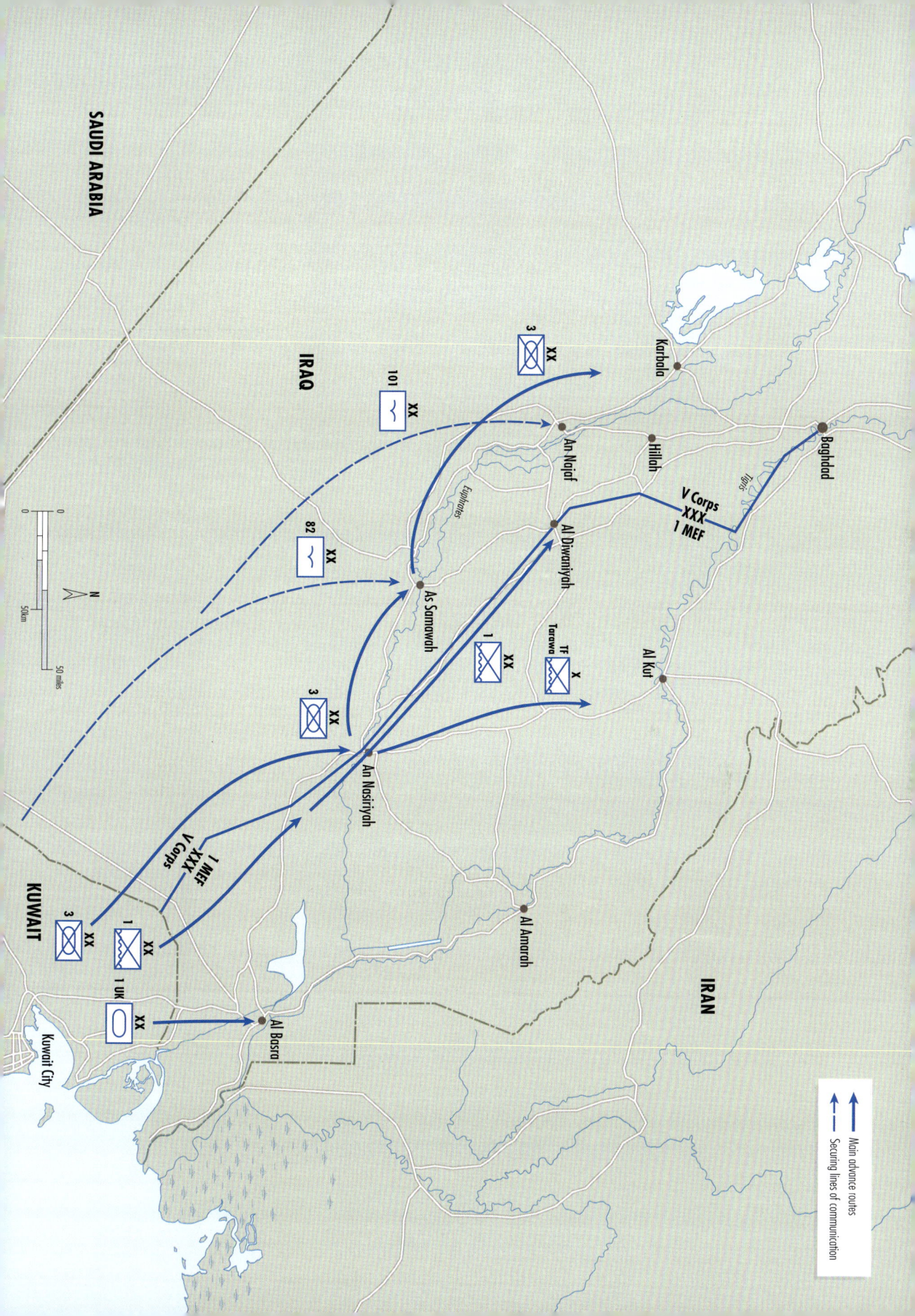

warships in the Red Sea. With no aerial opposition, the air war was to prove something of an anticlimax for the Coalition air defence crews.

Unfortunately, Coalition helicopters suffered more accidental losses in the morning of 22 March when two RN Westland Sea King ASuC7 Airborne Surveillance and Control helicopters collided at 0430hrs while transiting the northern Persian Gulf. Sadly, the accident was fatal and there were no survivors among the six British and one US personnel aboard the two aircraft.

The first Predator strike occurred later that day, when an MQ-1 Predator located an Iraqi ZSU-34/4 self-propelled anti-aircraft gun at 1325hrs near Al Amarah. The Predator destroyed it with an AGM-114K Hellfire II missile. Once again Firebee drones were used as decoys over Baghdad. On this night three Firebees dropped chaff while F-117 Nighthawks and B-2 Spirits conducted further airstrikes against targets within the Super-MEZ. More targets were hit by TLAMs launched from Coalition warships, with cruise missile strikes alternating through the night with manned aircraft attacks in order to keep the Iraqi air defences under continuous pressure. As well as the Firebee decoys, the attacks on Baghdad were supported by SEAD assets including F-16CJs and EA-6Bs. Two F-16CJs and two EA-6B Prowlers were tasked to support a B-1B Lancer, crewed by Lt Col Josef D Brown and Capts Lee Johnson, Steven Burgh and George Stone, which carried out four bomb runs to drop JDAMs accurately onto six GPS jammers which were deployed around Baghdad and which could potentially reduce the accuracy of satellite guided munitions. This B-1B was the first non-stealth aircraft to penetrate the Super-MEZ and it was subjected to heavy AAA fire as well as having four SAMs launched against it. Meanwhile other Coalition ground-attack aircraft continued the campaigns against the air defence system as well as against the depots and barracks of the Republican Guard. Missions included Tornado GR4s firing Storm Shadow missiles against the IOC at Al Taqaddum and Baghdad as well as command bunkers at Al Taqaddum and Al Asad.

A Tornado GR4 of 617 Sqn RAF, armed with two MBDA Storm Shadow missiles, starting engines at Ali Al Salem airbase, ready for a mission over Iraq on 22 March 2003. This was the combat debut of the Storm Shadow. (Crown Copyright/MoD)

For the first day of the campaign, the RAAF F/A-18 Hornets had been employed as defensive counter air for high value assets such as E-8s. Sortie lengths in this role were typically six hours. The aircraft were configured for air-to-air combat with AIM-9M Sidewinder and AIM-120 AMRAAM, but they also carried a single 500lb GBU-12 LGB in case they were needed for offensive support. On 22 March a pair of Hornets had been on defensive CAP for five hours when one aircraft was re-tasked to strike a time-sensitive ground target that had just been identified. After identifying the target, the pilot employed the GBU-12, the first bomb dropped in action by the RAAF since the Vietnam War.

In the western desert RAF Harriers flew five missions which included destroying two bridges near Ar Rutbah with LGBs. A-10s struck at IQAF aircraft that had been identified amongst defensive berms at H-2 airfield.

The night of 22/23 March was a busy one for SOF insertions. Firstly, at 2100hrs on 22 March, two Chinook HC2 helicopters had lifted from Arar airbase to insert a reconnaissance team from SOF TF 7 into a location near the Syrian border north of the Euphrates River. This team was to establish another tactical landing strip that would enable a larger infiltration by C-130 Hercules the following night. In a second mission that night, the team at Wadi Al Khirr had cleared the runway by the time the first flight of three pairs of Hercules, comprising USAF MC-130Hs and RAF C-130Ks, arrived at 20min intervals from 2200hrs, followed by another flight of six MC-130s at 0100hrs. The transports brought with them more SOF teams, who spread out into the desert. A third separate mission had started the previous night, when four MC-130H Combat Talons had set off from Mihail Kogălniceanu airport, near Constanta in Romania carrying the troops of Operational Detachment Alpha (ODA) 062. Their route took them across the eastern Mediterranean and the Sinai Peninsula to King Faisal airbase in Jordan where they rendezvoused with another pair of Combat Talons carrying the rest of the team. The six aircraft then took off at 2030hrs on 22 March and headed into Iraq, with the first three aircraft bound for Bashur airfield and the second three aiming for Sulaymaniyah. The routing for all six aircraft was a 590mi circuitous clockwise arc, tracking just inside the western and northern borders of Iraq. One mission planner, on seeing the route, had muttered 'that's one ugly baby' and the mission was henceforth known unofficially as Operation *Ugly Baby*. The route was flown at low level using NVG and TFR. As they headed towards Tal Afar, the aircraft came under heavy AAA fire and the last Combat Talon in the trail, captained by Maj Buck Haberichter, suffered a near miss from a 57mm shell, which blew out parts of the cockpit windshield, while hits from smaller calibre weapons took out the Number 2 engine. The damage was enough to force the crew to divert to Incirlik, but the other five aircraft reached their objectives successfully and delivered the SOF teams.

The Coalition suffered another aircraft loss, when an RAF Tornado GR4 from Ali Al Salem, which had been part of a large SEAD package supporting the interdiction missions, was shot down by the US Army at 0250hrs on 23 March. The Tornado was recovering to Ali Al Salem after completing its mission when it was engaged and destroyed by a Patriot SAM, killing the crew Flt Lts Kevin Main and David Williams.

By now the Coalition land forces had moved well into Iraq with 3rd Inf Div in control of the airbase at Tallil and its forward units continuing to push to the west of the Euphrates River past As Samawah towards An Najaf. On this day, Lt Col Dave Kennedy was tasked with preparing the runway at Tallil airbase for use as a forward operating base for Coalition CAS aircraft. With most of the operating surfaces in poor condition and sabotaged by the retreating Iraqis, this task would take four days. The air campaign now focussed primarily on supporting the advancing troops and also neutralizing the Republican Guard formations around Baghdad. The FSCL in the V Corps sector had been pushed out to a distance of 80mi ahead of the front lines, making it difficult for strike aircraft to engage targets anywhere near the line of contact. Instead, as it moved into contact with enemy forces,

Insertion of Special Operations Forces (SOF)

On the night of 21/22 March, SOF teams were inserted into three locations in Iraq.

EVENTS

1. 21–22 March: Four MC-130H Combat Talons arrive at King Faisal airbase from Mihail Kogălniceanu airbase, Romania carrying two battalions from 10 Special Forces Group, 2/10 and 3/30 SFG.

2. 2100hrs: Two RAF Chinooks operating from Arar insert SOF TF 7 to a position near the Syrian border.

3. 2200hrs: First flight of three pairs of Hercules, comprising USAF MC-130Hs and RAF C-130Ks, arrive at Wadi Al Khirr, which had been captured by SOF troops previously.

4. 2030hrs: Six Combat Talons take off from King Faisal airbase in two flights of three.

EVENTS

5. MC-130H flights cross into Iraq, flying at 150ft above the ground using NVGs.

6. Iraqi Anti-Aircraft Artillery fires at the Combat Talons.

7. Despite evasive manoeuvring, the Number 6 Combat Talon, callsign Harley 37, is hit and severely damaged. The crew decides to divert to Incirlik, Turkey.

8. The first three Combat Talons land at Bashur to insert 2/10 SFG.

9. The remaining two Combat Talons land at Sulaymaniyah and insert 3/10 SFG.

With no opposition from the IQAF, it was a relatively uneventful war for the Coalition air defence aircraft. Here, a Tornado F3 interceptor of 43 Squadron RAF awaits take-off clearance for a night Combat Air Patrol on 21 March 2003. (NARA)

the US Army relied mainly on its artillery and organic AH-64 Apaches to supplement its firepower. Meanwhile, 1 MARDIV and TF Tarawa were engaged in heavy fighting to capture the bridges over the Euphrates River at An Nasiriyah, closely supported by USMC AV-8s and RAF Harriers, along with USN and USMC F/A-18 Hornets as well as USAF F-16s and AC-130 Spookys which provided CAS where it was needed by the ground forces. They were also supported by organic AH-1W SuperCobra attack helicopters which often engaged targets 'danger close' in proximity to friendly forces. Unfortunately, during the battle for the An Nasiriyah bridges, one company from the TF Tarawa was deployed further forward than expected and when two A-10s were called in for CAS, the location of this unit was unknown to both the FAC and A-10 pilots. Despite taking time to clear their mission with the FAC, the A-10s (which were from the Pennsylvania Air National Guard) bombed and strafed the Marine position, killing a number of Marines. Throughout 23 March, a relay of USMC AFACs in F/A-18D Hornets, AV-8B Harriers and UH-1N Huey gunships and AH-1W SuperCobra attack helicopters coordinated USMC, USAF and RAF fixed-wing aircraft as they provided close support for the Marines fighting their way across the bridges. Equipped with the Litening II targeting pod, the AV-8B proved to be a particularly effective platform for armed reconnaissance and strike coordination, a mission more usually flown by the two-seat F/A-18D. By 1800hrs on 23 March, TF Tarawa was in control of the bridges at An Nasiriyah. CH-46 helicopters brought in resupplies and evacuated the wounded. On the same day, operations to shape the future battlefield south of Al Kut commenced. Marine AFAC F/A-18D Hornets flew armed reconnaissance missions around the town, co-ordinating strikes with other aircraft. These operations would continue daily for the next nine days.

From the outset of the campaign, the US Marines made good use of the P-3C Orions, which, thanks to their suite of high-resolution infrared and long-range electro-optical sensors and inverse synthetic aperture/synthetic aperture radar, gave the Marines valuable and timely information about what was ahead of them. The Orions were one part of an extensive surveillance and reconnaissance operation which informed both the ground and campaigns. The moving target indicator (MTI) sensors on Global Hawk and E-8 JSTARS, in addition to inputs from RC-135V/W Rivet Joint, tracked the movement of Iraqi ground forces. Some of these capabilities were duplicated by the RAF Nimrod fleet: both the R1 Elint and MR2 MPA variants operated with SOF teams during counter-TBM missions. Additional

An F-14D Tomcat launches from USS *Abraham Lincoln* (CVN 72) for a combat mission over Iraq on 21 March 2003. Superseded as an air defence fighter, the Tomcats were employed in both the strike and reconnaissance roles during the Iraq War. (NARA)

targeting information came from the fleet of seven RQ-1 Predators which patrolled much of Iraq. Daily tactical reconnaissance sorties by Tornado GR4s using RAPTOR and F-14D Tomcats using TARPS assisted with battle damage assessment, which fed back to the targeting cells at the CAOC to ensure that missions were not wasted against targets that had already been successfully struck. Furthermore, aircraft over Iraq were controlled by E-3 AWACS, or in some cases carrier-borne E-2 Hawkeyes, which could re-direct strike aircraft to higher priority targets if needed. Once it was clear that IQAF fighters did not present a threat and SEAD efforts had effectively neutralized most of the SAM sites, E-3 and E-8 orbits moved further north into Iraqi airspace, increasing their cover of the operational area. Coordination of the air support for 1 MEF was carried out by a relay of three KC-130 command and control aircraft, which fulfilled much the same role as the E-3 over the rest of Iraq. In particular, the KC-130 was able to maintain communications with USMC helicopters, something that the USMC had found difficult previously because the ground-based command centre lost line of sight communication with low flying aircraft.

As the forward edge of the battle advanced northwards, it began to move beyond the unrefuelled range of most tactical aircraft. By this stage of the conflict some 1,400 AAR tanker sorties were being flown per day, but even this level of effort could not meet the needs of all aircraft. The carrier-based aircraft were particularly hard hit and the USN felt that its requirements were not being given sufficient priority. However, a partial solution was found in using the F/A-18E Super Hornets, as well as the S-3B

Storm Shadow in combat

In the early hours of 22 March 2003, Tornado GR4 crew Sqn Ldr Andrew M Myers and Wg Cdr David Robertson (commanding 617 Squadron) launched two Storm Shadow missiles from a position west of Baghdad at an air defence radar facility near Kirkuk. Robertson recalled that 'There was a lot of AAA visible around every town when amplified by night vision goggles (NVG) and as we approached Baghdad, the sky seemed to be alight with AAA and missiles'. The image depicts the aircraft just after it had launched the second of its two Storm Shadow missiles, near Lake Habbaniyah to the west of Baghdad.

Vikings, as organic AAR tankers. The situation was eased slightly when the Turkish government granted overflight clearance to Coalition aircraft on 24 March, allowing direct transit into northern Iraq by tankers based in Romania and Cyprus. The lack of AAR tankers was just one frustration: often radio communications were swamped by sheer volume and sometimes aircraft that were waiting to be called forward became fuel critical before they could be employed. The unwieldy CAS allocation system used by V Corps also complicated matters, and it was not infrequent for aircraft to return to base with unexpended ordnance. This caused a further problem because weapons had a 'shelf life' of limited hours, so time-expired weapons had to be stored and disposed of; further resupplies of weapons were also needed.

On the night of 23/24 March and through the next day, US aircraft flew around 2,000 sorties of which over 800 were offensive action, including 500 sorties against pre-planned targets. TLAM strikes and F-117 Nighthawk and B-2 Spirit attacks against targets in Baghdad continued through the night. Four F/A-18C Hornets from VMFA-323 aboard USS *Constellation* attacked the Special Republican Guard barracks and presidential security buildings near Saddam International Airport with 2,000lb JDAMs. As on the previous nights, Coalition SEAD missions limited the Iraqi SAM crews to firing missiles ballistically, so they were little threat to the attacking aircraft. Nevertheless, numerous SAMs were launched, and Iraqi AAA gunners also kept up a heavy but inaccurate barrage of fire. In their new swing role, RAAF F/A-18 Hornets participated in a pre-planned strike on a Republican Guard facility near Al Kut.

Late on 23 March, the Apache attack helicopters of the US Army 11th Aviation Regiment prepared for a deep strike mission against the Republican Guard Medina Division which was located between Najaf and Baghdad. Originally the mission had been planned for 48 helicopters, but a shortage of fuel at the Forward Arming and Refuel Point (FARP) because of transport difficulties on the roads meant that the attack would have to be conducted by

Air-to-air refuelling was the critical component of the air campaign over Iraq. The KC-10A Extender, seen here taxiing to the parking ramp after an OIF mission on 22 March 2003, was equipped with both a boom and a hose, so it could refuel all the Coalition aircraft types. (NARA)

fewer aircraft. The reduced force of 31 AH-64D Apaches and one UH-60 Black Hawk command helicopter deployed to a FARP at Objective Rams, just west of An Najaf. However, the mission was doomed almost from the start: firstly, the ingress route past Najaf, which was thought to be empty desert, was in fact a well-defended suburbia, and secondly a *shamal* dust storm began to cover the area during the evening which made flying conditions difficult. In particular, it grounded the IAI/AAI RQ-2A Pioneer UAVs that should have given accurate updated target coordinates for the helicopter crews. Thirdly, although SEAD support had been arranged, a delay to the take-off time because of the weather was not passed on to the fixed-wing SEAD aircraft, with the result that there were no longer any suitable aircraft airborne by the time that the helicopters took off for the mission. The weather conditions were not good at Objective Rams and most pilots had experienced 'brown-out' as they touched down. Nevertheless, the Apaches set off at 0115hrs on 24 March, although one aircraft was written off when it crashed on take-off after the crew became disorientated in the brown-out conditions. The remaining 30 gunships, accompanied by the Regimental CO Col William T Wolf in the Black Hawk, pressed on, with the crews flying on NVGs. As the Apaches passed An Najaf, the lights in all the surrounding towns and villages were simultaneously switched off for a few seconds, apparently a warning to Iraqi forces further north of the approaching helicopters. The Apaches were almost instantly met with a hail of fire, the tracer from small arms and larger AAA lighting the sky so brightly that NVGs were dazzled. The Apaches were particularly vulnerable when they had to climb to cross power cables, obstacles which were unexpected on the route. One of the first Apaches, flown by CWO2 John Tomblin and 1st Lt Jason King was badly hit, and King received a bullet through his throat causing the crew to abort the mission. During the mission, all of the Apaches were hit by AAA fire: most of them were badly damaged and one helicopter, flown by CWOs David S Young and Ronald D Young, was shot down. Lt Col Daniel Ball, the CO of 1-227 Attack Helicopter Battalion attempted to cover the crew as they tried to evade capture, but his Apache was severely mauled and he had to withdraw, leaving the crew to be taken as prisoners of war. With no accurate target update and flying in marginal conditions against well dispersed vehicles in defensive berms, the Apache crews had great difficulty in finding targets for their Hellfire missiles. The modest achievement of destroying a dozen Iraqi vehicles was bought at the cost of severe damage to some 30 helicopters and the complete loss of two more.

The weather closes in

On 24 March, 800 sorties were flown by Coalition aircraft against 'targets of opportunity', indicating a shift from pre-planned interdiction missions to CAS for ground troops. Offensive support aircraft were now tasked into KICAS boxes. However, while KICAS boxes beyond the FSCL were relatively easy to service, deteriorating weather conditions with the onset of the *shamal* made CAS difficult when neither FAC nor aircrew could see their targets. SEAD efforts continued, but once again, it was the US Army air defences that proved the greatest danger to Coalition aircraft; at about 1540hrs a Patriot radar locked onto a USAF F-16CJ which was some 30mi south of An Najaf. The F-16 pilot responded by firing an AGM-88 HARM which hit the radar. Fortunately, there were no casualties from this engagement. During the day an EC-130E Commando Solo detachment under command of Lt Col Gerald E Otterbein deployed into theatre. The Commando Solo crews were soon exercising their ability to broadcast television transmissions on Iraqi TV channels and radio broadcast on AM/FM/HF radios including interrupting civilian radio programmes and net intrusion onto Iraqi military frequencies.

The two USN aircraft carriers in the Mediterranean, USS *Harry S Truman* and *Theodore Roosevelt*, were sailing just off the Nile Delta. Their aircraft were playing a full part in operations, flying south over the Sinai Peninsula to enter Saudi airspace then turning north

An F/A-18 Hornet of 75 Squadron RAAF refuels during an OIF mission. During the Iraq War, the RAAF F/A-18 Hornets flew 350 combat missions, armed in the offensive support role with 500lb GBU-12 LGBs. (T van Haren)

to carry out missions in the west and north of Iraq. On 24 March aircraft from *Harry S Truman* attacked SA-2 and Roland SAM sites near Kirkuk with HARM. At 0220hrs that morning, two RAF Chinook HC2s extracted the reconnaissance team from TF7 which had been compromised shortly after its insertion two days previously. The extraction was covered by a pair of F-16s.

On 25 March ground operations in Iraq were brought to a halt as the *shamal* took hold, bringing high winds and reducing visibility to zero over most of southern Iraq. Army and Marine attack helicopters were grounded, and poor conditions also limited the flying from some of the airfields in the region. Nevertheless, the air component flew some 1,400 combat and combat support missions over Iraq on 25 March. Much of the responsibility for offensive support fell to the carrier-based aircraft in the Persian Gulf and those in the Eastern Mediterranean Sea. Laser guidance for weapons became impossible, making the CAOC insist on JDAM or EPW loadouts. Since CAS had become problematic, the CAOC planners took the opportunity to strike the 3,000 known fixed military sites, being an assortment of revetments, defensive areas and ammunition storage facilities. To ensure that empty locations were not needlessly attacked, each potential target was checked electronically by JSTARS, Rivet Joint, U-2S and/or Onyx satellite to identify those that should be hit. The positions of the three Republican Guard divisions, the Medina Al Nina and Hammurabi Armoured Divisions, were also targeted. The bombardment would last from nightfall on 25 March through to the morning of 27 March, involving B-1B, B-52, F-15E and Tornado GR4 aircraft. The Iraqi soldiers, who thought that they would be safe under cover of the *shamal* were shocked that the weather conditions offered no sanctuary from the attentions of Coalition aircraft and desertion rates amongst Iraqi military units soared.

When the *shamal* halted the ground advance, soldiers of the US Army 3rd Squadron 7th Cavalry (3-7 Cav) found themselves isolated on the enemy side of the Euphrates at Abu Sukhayr, just south of An Najaf. Under cover of the sandstorm, Iraqi forces including irregulars began assaulting their positions in a battle that lasted two days. During this

A derivative of the C-130 Hercules transport aircraft and designed specifically for infiltration, exfiltration and resupply of Special Operations Forces (SOF) in hostile territory, the MC-130H Combat Talon was operated by the 7th Special Operations Squadron during OIF. (USAF)

time, the FAC, Staff Sgt Michael S Shropshire, called in hundreds of JDAM strikes. In one incident, after being advised by an E-8C JSTARS of the approach of an Iraqi armoured column, Shropshire called in a B-1B which dropped 12 JDAMs, destroying ten T-72 tanks.

There was little SAM activity from the Iraqis, but aircraft that descended to lower levels, such as A-10s carrying out CAS, were greeted by heavy and often accurate AAA fire. On 25 March two F/A-18C Hornets from VFA-151 aboard USS *Constellation* were called in to attack time sensitive Iraqi naval targets on the Shatt-al-Arab near Basra. The Hornets engaged an Osa I-class missile boat and a training vessel on the river. Meanwhile, a S-3B Viking was diverted to strike the Presidential yacht *Al Mansur* which was being used by the Iraqi forces in the area as a command centre. The target was laser-illuminated by one of the Hornets while the Viking fired an AGM-65E Maverick, which scored a direct hit on the yacht. This was a double first for the S-3B – the first time that the Viking had fired a Maverick in combat and the first time that the aircraft had been used for an overland strike mission.

Despite the poor weather, fighting also continued around An Nasiriyah as TF Tarawa sought to hold the bridges over the Euphrates River and Saddam Canal and to eject enemy forces from the town. The Marines were supported by SOF teams from TF20, which infiltrated the city to locate Fedayeen and Ba'ath Party positions, and then called in JDAM or AC-130U Spooky airstrikes to neutralize these targets. Further south, RAF Harrier GR7s bombed the Ba'ath Party headquarters in Az Zubayr, some 12mi south of Basra.

Just before midnight on 26 March the US Army 173rd Airborne Brigade conducted a large-scale parachute drop on Bashur airfield. The airfield had been prepared previously by the SOF team ODA 062 on 23 March. Fifteen C-17 Globemasters carried 954 paratroopers and their equipment from Aviano airbase in Italy to make the drop. The first five Globemasters carried High Mobility Multipurpose Wheeled Vehicles (HMMWV 'Humvees') and weapons, while the remaining ten aircraft carried the paratroops. At 30,000ft the C-17s flew a route that made use of the recently granted permission to use Turkish airspace and were escorted in Iraqi airspace by USN F/A-18s. The drop itself was made from 1,000ft, with the C-17 pilots flying on NVGs. A few hours later in the western desert, early on 27 March, paratroops

The prime mission of the RAF Chinook force during the Iraq War was to carry out infiltration and exfiltration of British SOF troops. The rugged conditions experienced by helicopter in the desert are well illustrated in this image. (Crown Copyright/MoD)

of A Company, 3rd Battalion 75th Rangers along with engineers from B Company, 27th Engineer Battalion and their heavy equipment jumped from three more C-17s to seize the airfield at H-1. After the Rangers secured the objective, the engineers set to removing the rock piles and tank hulks which the Iraqis had used to block the runways. The task was completed and the first aircraft to land, an MC-130, touched down just five hours after the initial parachute drop. The airfield was then used as a forward base to support land operations around the Haditha Dam. In a similar timescale, a group of five C-130 Hercules, made up of two KC-130s from VMGR-452 and three C-130Ks from 70 Squadron RAF, landed using NVGs onto the abandoned airfield at Jalibah, some 40mi south-east of An Nasiriyah. The RAF aircraft carried much needed resupplies of rations, water and artillery ammunition, while the US aircraft carried aviation fuel into Jalibah, and evacuated wounded Marines on the return leg. Further resupplies on subsequent days would be made onto a highway strip which was to be established as a FARP on an 8,000ft section of the Shaikh Hantush Highway, some 15mi north of Ad Diwaniyah.

The sandstorm lasted into 27 March. Despite the low visibility, Iraqi forces continued to mount attacks against US Army positions near An Najaf, USMC positions near An Nasiriyah and British positions near Basra. However, CAS by Coalition aircraft took their toll of Iraqi personnel and equipment, often neutralizing the threat before it could close on Coalition positions. The campaign against Iraqi air defences also continued, with at least three SAM sites bombed. These strikes were supported by a HARM-loaded EA-6B Prowler from VQ-131, which ensured that the radars were shut down. In the south-east of the country, Iraqi forces were still typically firing one TBM (an Ababil-100 or Al-Samoud missile) towards Kuwait each day. The missiles were invariably intercepted by Patriot SAMs long before they reached their objective, and the launchers were vulnerable to Coalition aircraft which mounted patrols close to areas where launches were taking place. One launcher was destroyed in this way by an A-10 on 27 March.

Meanwhile the counter-TBM operations in the western desert were frustrated by the weather, although some armed reconnaissance sorties were flown and a Nimrod MR2 was tasked into Iraqi airspace for the first time to search the area to the south and east of Ar Rutbah. In response to a request for air support from an Australian SOF unit, two B-2 Spirits dropped 23 JDAMs on a radio transmitter tower near Al Nukhayb.

In the south-east, RAF Harrier GR7s flew eight missions against Iraqi forces located at Al Amarah, Al Kut, Karbala, Hillah and Ad Diwaniyah. Tornado GR4s from Al Udeid successfully attacked the Republican Guard barracks in Ramadi and also the Republican Guard fuel depot at Numaniyah, while Tornados from Ali Al Salem tasked with KICAS bombed armoured vehicles near Ad Diwaniyah. That evening at 2300hrs a B-2 Spirit dropped two precision-guided 4,500lb GBU-37 'bunker buster' bombs onto the Iraqi government communication tower on the eastern bank of the Tigris River in central Baghdad. This strike was part of the wider efforts to sever links between the Iraqi central command and its subordinate units.

More TBM launchers were destroyed the following afternoon, when two F/A-18C Hornets located three Al-Samoud launchers approximately 25mi north-west of Basra. With a clearance in the weather, Coalition aircraft targeted Republican Guard units and Ba'ath Party facilities. Two F-15E Strike Eagles bombed the Ba'ath Party barracks in Basra with 2,000lb LGBs, killing some 200 paramilitary personnel who were using the site. RAF Tornado GR4s launched two Storm Shadow missiles at each of the cable switch bunkers at Taji and Al Taqaddum airfields. Four more Tornado GR4s on a KICAS mission were tasked by a RQ-1 Predator UAV against armoured vehicles sheltering in a treeline near Ad Diwaniyah. A USN AFAC marked the target area with a white phosphorous rocket, after which the Tornados dropped RBL755 cluster munitions onto the enemy vehicles. Even under FAC control, a perennial problem with CAS missions was identifying targets correctly and discriminating between friendly and enemy vehicles. On 28 March an A-10 Thunderbolt misidentified four British AFVs as Iraqi and strafed them with its 30mm cannon, killing one trooper and wounding five others.

Further to the north, there was a steady flow of personnel and equipment into Bashur airfield: from 28 March, 12 C-17 Globemasters flew into the airfield each day, bringing another 1,200 troops into theatre. The improved weather also meant that the RAF Canberra PR9s based at Azraq could continue with their high-level photoreconnaissance missions over western Iraq: three such missions were flown daily. Harriers operating from Azraq attacked two hardened shelters on the disused airfield at Ar Rutbah, to the north-west of the H-2 airbase. Five more pairs of Harriers carried out armed reconnaissance sorties searching for TBM launchers.

Late in the afternoon, a 250-vehicle convoy of USMC aviation ground support elements was ambushed on Highway 7 near Ash Shatrah as it headed to set up a new FARP at Qalat Sikar. Four AH-1W SuperCobras responded to the initial call for air support as dusk fell but were very short of fuel. The

When the *shamal* conditions halted the Coalition ground advance, the troops became reliant on air support from aircraft like this B-1B Lancer, seen here during an OIF mission on 25 March 2003. The impressive weapon load, including JDAM, and extended loiter time of the B-1B made it an exceptionally good CAS platform. (NARA)

Marines improvised a hot-refuelling site alongside the convoy, enabling the Cobras to stay on station and give the necessary fire support. The helicopters were also joined by F/A-18 Hornets. Between them, the Hornets and Cobras flew 12 CAS sorties through the night.

Learning from its previous experience, the 11th Aviation Regiment carried out another deep strike Apache mission against the Medina Division of the Republican Guard. It was carried out by two battalions, totalling just under 50 aircraft, flying from two new FARPs to the south-west of An Najaf. After take-off just after 2200hrs, one battalion flew due north directly to the target area on Highway 9 just south of Karbala, while the other approached from over the Razzaza Lake. This time the route avoided populated areas, and the helicopters were preceded by an artillery SEAD strike with MGM-140 Army Tactical Missile System (ATACMS) as well as by fixed-wing aircraft providing further SEAD cover and mounting diversionary attacks. Rather than directly engaging targets en-route and thereby using up their own weapons before reaching the designated target, the Apache pilots were briefed to call in any enemy positions to Lt Col Stephen Smith in an accompanying UH-60 Black Hawk. He would then liaise with AWACS to send fixed-wing aircraft to deal with the target. Unfortunately, in practice the communication with the AWACS controller proved problematic and Smith resorted to calling on Guard frequency for support. This was forthcoming in the shape of a pair of F/A-18 Hornets which neutralized an anti-aircraft site. Other aircraft in the vicinity included a flight of RAF Tornado GR4s which engaged armoured vehicles under direction of an AFAC. The Apaches attacked in pairs, with one helicopter making the Hellfire missile attack while the other gave covering fire with its gun; the pair then made a second pass, swapping roles. Overall, the mission fared much better than the previous attempt and only two helicopters were damaged. However, the final score of just six APCs, four tanks and five trucks was disappointing.

The effects of a *shamal* sandstorm which closed many of the airfields in the region can be seen shrouding these F-16CJ aircraft from the 77th Fighter Squadron on 26 March 2003. (NARA)

The forward line of engagement for US V Corps now ran along the line of the Euphrates River between An Najaf and Karbala. At this stage, Gen McKiernan called a brief halt to the advance in order to resupply the front-line units before the advance towards Baghdad. During the day of 29 March, Iraqi forces carried out a reconnaissance of part of the 3rd Inf Div form-up areas using at least two propeller-driven ultralight aircraft. Although the aircraft were detected, the anti-aircraft units in the area were unable to get authority to fire on them before they flew off. The aircraft were most likely flown by members of a paramilitary organization. To the east, TF Tarawa continued its mission to clear An Nasiriyah, finding that the AH-1W SuperCobra was also a particularly effective weapon system in the urban environment. In addition, the leading echelons of 1 MARDIV advanced past Qalat Sukar, some 50mi further north. Meanwhile, in northern Iraq, Coalition aircraft bombed Iraqi positions at Chamchal near Kirkuk, prior to a successful assault by Kurdish *peshmerga* forces.

The air campaign rolled on with further airstrikes against targets in the Baghdad area. RAF Tornado GR4s from Ali Al Salem launched four Storm Shadow missiles against the Defence Ministry buildings in Baghdad and one further Storm Shadow was released against a communications bunker on the airbase at Kirkuk. Tornados from Ali Al Salem and Al Udeid also carried out a number of strikes on the Republican Guard barracks at Shaykh Mazhar, some 25mi south-east of Baghdad. The 3 MAW took advantage of the pause in ground movement to shape the battlefield in front of 1 MARDIV, conducting numerous airstrikes against the Republican Guard Baghdad Division near Al Kut and against Iraqi regular units near Al Amarah and Basra. AFACs in F/A-18Ds carried out armed reconnaissance sorties and directed attacks, many of which were carried out by the USMC F/A-18 units. In the western desert, A-10 Thunderbolts engaged Iraqi ground targets, and Harrier GR7s bombed support buildings at H-2 prior to an assault by SOF. Aircraft also engaged an Iraqi armoured unit that had moved onto the eastern bank of the Euphrates River near the Haditha Dam.

Marine wing support personnel refuel USMC F/A-18C Hornets at Al Jaber airbase, Kuwait on 26 March 2003. Two AV-8B Harriers can be seen in the background and the reduction in visibility caused by the *shamal* is apparent. (NARA)

Cloud over southern Iraq prevented some missions from delivering weapons during 30 March. However, a strike package which included B-1B Lancer, B-2A Spirit and B-52H Stratofortress bombers flew JDAM attacks against targets in Baghdad. The targets included two of the SA-2 sites that ringed Baghdad, a command and communications hub at the Abu Ghurayb presidential palace (immediately east of Saddam International Airport), two facilities in the Karrada Intelligence Service complex (on the banks of the Tigris River in south Baghdad) and the Fedayeen training centre at Ar Rustamiyah (in the southern outskirts of the city). Multiple TLAMs also struck the Information Ministry buildings. A total of 1,200 precision-guided bombs and 14 TLAMs were expended during the course of the day.

Both RAF and USMC Harriers were also active over the south and east during the day. A pair of RAF Harrier GR7s led by Flt Lt Ian Townsend demolished a communications mast south of the capital with EPW, and a pair of USMC AV-8Bs flown by Captains Guy G Berry and Gregory Warrington of VMFA-211 fought off Iraqi infantry that was moving towards a UH-1 Huey that had force-landed with engine trouble. The AV-8Bs kept the Iraqi troops away from the helicopter until a rescue of the downed crew could be effected.

Four Super Hornets, comprising two F/A-18Es flown by Lt Cdrs Hal Schmitt and Jason Norris, and two F/A-18Fs flown by Lt Cdrs Brian Garrison and Mark Weisgerber and Lts Tom Poulter and Tom Bodine, launched from the USS *Nimitz* in the Strait of Malacca on 30 March to fly via Diego Garcia to the *Abraham Lincoln*. Their journey consisted of two legs of over 2,000mi each. The transfer was made so that the Super Hornets could act as extra AAR tankers for CVW-14 aboard the USS *Abraham Lincoln*.

The AAR tanker towlines in the west moved northwards into Iraqi airspace for the first time, a move which meant that aircraft could remain on station for longer periods of time.

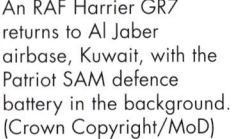

An RAF Harrier GR7 returns to Al Jaber airbase, Kuwait, with the Patriot SAM defence battery in the background. (Crown Copyright/MoD)

Harriers carried out armed reconnaissance missions searching for TBM launchers and also carried out overwatch for a SOF team working near Ar Rutbah. One pair of Harriers was directed to contact an RQ-1 Predator operator who tasked the aircraft against a Roland SAM launcher that had been detected on the airfield at Al Asad. After the Harrier pilots experienced some difficulty in identifying the target, the Predator used its laser designator to mark the target, which was then successfully attacked with an EPW II.

That night the SOF troops of TF 7 were compromised by a large well-armed Iraqi unit and an emergency extraction was called. TF 7 managed to break contact with the enemy force and withdrew towards H-1 airfield which had been captured by TF 20. Two RAF Chinooks were supported by two C-130K Hercules which carried fuel so that the Chinooks could refuel at H-1 before the homebound leg, while a flight of F-16s provided overwatch. A pair of Harriers which was already on a different task was also diverted to support the operation. In fact, TF 7 had been split into four well-dispersed groups, and it took some time for the Chinooks and F-16s to locate three of the groups. Another pair of Chinooks was dispatched to locate and evacuate the fourth group. Despite being locked up by Iraqi radars, the Chinooks eventually found the missing team, although the lead Chinook mistook the strobe light used by the SOF team as enemy gunfire and returned fire until the wingman advised them of the error. Fortunately, no-one was injured in the incident.

Early on the morning of 31 March, Lt Col Michael K Hile led four sections of AV-8B Harriers from the USS *Bonhomme Richard* on a mission in support of a predawn raid into Ash Shatrah, which lies some 25mi north of An Nasiriyah. The targets were a cluster of eight buildings near to the Ba'ath Party headquarters in the town. The Harriers were to attack using 500lb bombs with laser guidance from the Litening II targeting pod, to minimize collateral damage and reduce the chance of hitting friendly forces who were positioned close by. The mission was completed successfully and during the raid the Marines captured several Ba'ath Party members as well as weapons caches and documents.

During the day some 2,000 missions were flown by Coalition air forces, including 800 attack missions and 400 AAR missions. Approximately two-thirds of the strike missions were targeted against the Republican Guard Medina, Baghdad and Hammurabi Divisions.

Much of the close air support task both for the Coalition main force and the counter-TBM forces was flown by A-10A Thunderbolts. Some 60 A-10s, which had been designed from the outset for the CAS role, took part in the Iraq War. (NARA)

OPPOSITE COALITION GROUND CAMPAIGN NORTHERN IRAQ, APRIL 2003

A B-2 Spirit recovering to Diego Garcia after a mission over Iraq on 27 March 2003. The aircraft flew 20-hour sorties from their home station at Whitman airbase, Missouri staging through Diego Garcia on their return after they had carried out the mission over Iraq. (NARA)

At around 0500hrs, the Baghdad Exchange Maidan communications facility in central Baghdad was bombed with 2,000lb precision-guided bombs. AC-130U Spooky gunships also operated against regime targets as well as targets of opportunity. Other targets attacked by Coalition aircraft during the day included the Iraqi TV transmitter in Karbala and the Ba'ath Party headquarters in Al Hillah. More targets in Baghdad were struck by the heavy bombers, including a command-and-control complex in eastern Baghdad.

Meanwhile Coalition ground forces regained the offensive and, in the V Corps area, the 3rd Inf Div seized the bridge over the Euphrates at Al Hindiyah, while the 101st Airborne Div captured An Najaf airfield. In the west, the SOF troops of TF20 were rapidly redeployed from H-1 to capture the Haditha Dam; this was to prevent the possibility of the dam being destroyed by the nearby Iraqi armoured unit. In the north of the country, aircraft from CVW-8 aboard the USS *Theodore Roosevelt* in the Mediterranean Sea flew over 40 missions in support of the 173rd Airborne Brigade against Iraqi military targets, including artillery batteries, a barracks and a SAM site.

Late in the evening, the first KC-130 Hercules began to land on the Shaikh Hantush Highway strip near Ad Diwaniyah, to deliver supplies and aviation fuel to 1 MARDIV. The repaired runway at Tallil airbase was now available thanks to the efforts of Lt Col Kennedy and his team, and it was used for the first time by A-10 Thunderbolts on 31 March.

The advance to Baghdad

Throughout 1 April the Republican Guard Baghdad Division opposite 1 MARDIV and the Republican Guard Medina Division facing 3rd Inf Div came under heavy air and land attack. As a result, these divisions were estimated by US intelligence to have lost 75 to 85 per cent of their combat capability. The Republican Guard Hammurabi and Al Nida Divisions were also subjected to heavy aerial bombardment. B-52 Stratofortresses dropped CBU-15 Sensor Fused Weapons for the first time; these weapons were GPS guided to the aiming point, after which submunitions with IR sensors were dispensed. Meanwhile, Tornado GR4s engaged targets south-east of Baghdad under direction of an F-15E Strike Eagle AFAC. Psychological operations were also mounted against Iraqi military forces, including broadcasts by the four EC-130E Commando Solos which were now in theatre.

During the day there was continuous air activity over the Haditha Dam, where TF20 was the subject of vigorous counterattacks by a strong Iraqi force. A pair of Harrier GR7s attempted unsuccessfully to engage three patrol boats on the reservoir but they were successful

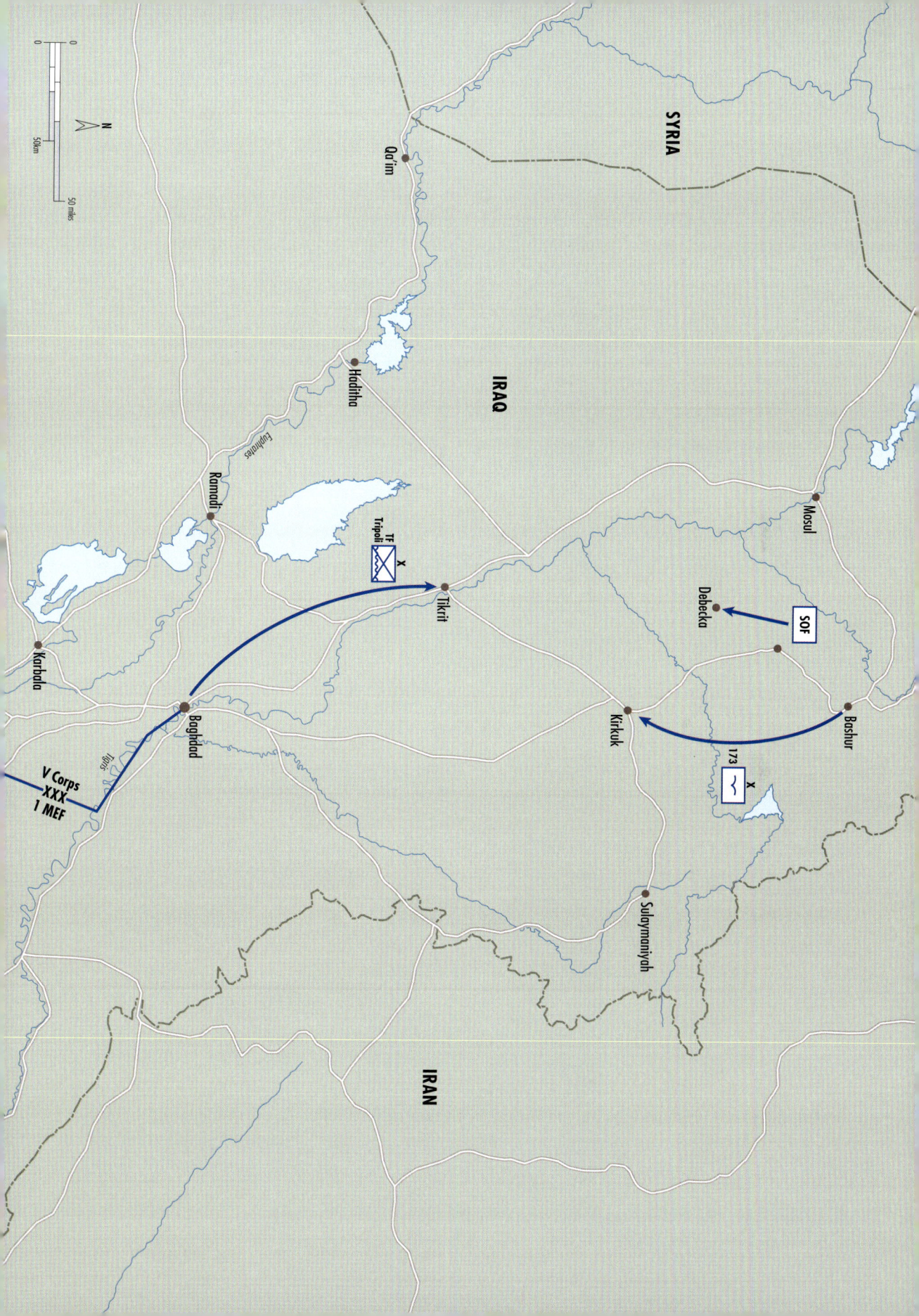

in neutralizing a nearby artillery position. The boats were destroyed by a second pair of Harriers, before a formation of F-16s arrived on scene and took over responsibility for CAS. A-10 Thunderbolts were also busy providing CAS for the defenders of the dam.

There were two aircraft losses on 1 April, neither of which was related to enemy action. In the first, an S-3B Viking slid off the deck of USS *Constellation* after a successful landing at 0510hrs. The aircraft had suffered a hydraulic failure rendering the brakes ineffective and the Viking rolled over the side of the deck as it attempted to taxi to its parking area. Both pilots ejected successfully. In the other accident, which occurred that evening at 1940hrs, an AV-8B Harrier crashed into the Persian Gulf while recovering to USS *Nassau*. The pilot ejected safely and was recovered.

Just after midnight on 1 April a rescue mission was launched to recover Private Jessica D Lynch, a US prisoner of war who was being held in the hospital in An Nasiriyah. She had been captured when the US Army supply convoy had been ambushed near An Nasiriyah on 23 March. Subsequently, an Iraqi informer had told US Marines of her location, making a rescue attempt possible. While other units mounted a diversionary attack to draw Iraqi forces away from the hospital, a SOF rescue team was inserted by a ten-helicopter formation of CH-46E Sea Knights and CH-53E Super Stallions. The helicopters were in turn covered by AC-130 Spookys, A-10 Thunderbolts and AV-8B Harriers. The Litening II targeting pod on one AV-8B was used to stream live video footage to the battle staff in the CAOC. Lynch was successfully located in the hospital and evacuated by helicopter. Meanwhile under SOF direction, aircraft destroyed various buildings and vehicles in An Nasiriyah, including bombing the headquarters of the director general of security in the region.

Early on 2 April 3rd Inf Div advanced northwards and penetrated the Karbala Gap, between Lake Razzaza and Karbala, easily pushing through the remnants of the Republican Guard positions. 1 MARDIV crossed the Tigris River at Al Kut. The Tigris River then became the boundary between 1 MEF and V Corps. Coalition ground forces were supported by over 900 attack missions flown throughout the day. Unfortunately, during a sortie south of Baghdad an F-15E Strike Eagle crew misidentified a US Army M270 Multiple Launch Rocket System (MLRS) battery as a SAM battery and bombed it, killing three soldiers and wounding five more. The air tasking during the day included missions against command-

Although it was primarily a maritime patrol aircraft, the Nimrod MR2, like this example seen on 27 March 2003, was used extensively by the RAF in the ISTAR role in support of SOF operations. (NARA)

and-control facilities in and around Baghdad, including a command-and-control facility at Radwaniyah which was bombed with JDAMs. At 2200hrs Coalition aircraft also dropped 40 JDAMs onto a supply depot in the Al Karkh district of Baghdad that was used by the Special Republican Guard and Special Security Organization. RAF Harriers were in action over Basra as British forces continued to clear the city of Iraqi forces.

The TF 20 remained in control of the Haditha Dam, but Iraqi forces contested the dam throughout the day. An F-14A Tomcat was lost in the early hours while supporting TF20 near the dam. The aircraft, which was operating from Al Udeid, suffered an engine failure and fuel transfer problems at around 0150hrs. The crew, Lt Chad P Vincelette and Lt Cdr Scotty McDonald, ejected safely and were lucky that their survival beacons were picked up by an overhead U-2S Dragon Lady which reported the contact to the National Reconnaissance Office (NRO) in California. The NRO in turn alerted the CAOC and a rescue mission was initiated with two HH-60G Pave Hawk helicopters led by Maj Chris Barnett scrambled from their base in Jordan. The helicopters rendezvoused with a flight of A-10s led by the on-scene mission commander, Maj Jim Stephenson who directed the rescue and helped to locate the downed crew members. As dawn broke over the dam, Iraqi attacks on the position intensified. There was virtually continuous air action over the dam during through the day, with numerous aircraft in the area awaiting tasking. A-10s were called in to strike Iraqi artillery and mortar positions. RAF Harrier GR7s also joined the fray: Wg Cdr Stuart Atha and Flt Lt James A Schofield engaged Iraqi artillery positions with EPW LGBs and a Maverick missile. At the request of the FAC, Harriers also destroyed a building that was being used by Iraqi troops.

There were two more aircraft losses on 2 April. First, an MH-60L Black Hawk DAP crashed in the vicinity of Karbala at 1930hrs, killing seven of the 11 personnel on board. Then, in another blue-on-blue incident a US Army Patriot battery shot down an F/A-18C Hornet from USS *Kitty Hawk* as it returned from a strike mission north of Karbala 2330hrs. The pilot, Lt Nathan D White was killed, and the wreckage of the aircraft fell into Lake Razzaza.

C-17 Globemaster III transports on the ramp at Aviano airbase, Italy. Fifteen Globemasters carried airborne troops to northern Iraq for the combat parachute drop on Bashur airfield on 26 March 2003. (USAF)

On the night of 2/3 April an SOF Team carried out a raid on one of Saddam Hussein's palaces, the Tharthar Palace on the south-eastern end of Lake Tharthar some 50mi northwest of Baghdad. Access to the palace had been denied to the UNSCOM team before the war and it was thought that WMDs might be stored there. An assault force of four MH-47E Chinook, four MH-60L Black Hawk DAPs and two MH-60K Black Hawks would be supported by five MC-130E Combat Talons and three MC-130P Combat Shadows for AAR. The whole package would be escorted by A-10 Thunderbolts and be supported by F-14D Tomcats, F-15E Strike Eagles, F-16CJ and EA-6B Prowlers, making an overall force of some 60 aircraft. After setting off from Ali Al Salem, the C-130Es refuelled at Arar, but one aircraft became unserviceable, leaving two pairs. The Combat Talons were to conduct the pre-infiltration AAR after which the lead pair, captained by Lt Col Kenneth E Ray and Maj James Winsmann, would reposition close to the target in order to top up the gunship helicopters. During the initial AAR bracket, the lead pair were fired on by SAMs and the leader of the second pair, flown by Maj Bruce R Taylor, was also fired on by a suspected SA-8 SAM. The helicopters disengaged from the tankers and dispensed flares, which successfully countered the missiles but also had the effect of washing out the NVGs that the pilots were using. Notwithstanding these difficulties the landing was successful, although another SAM was fired at the Combat Talons as they loitered in the target area. During the exfiltration, the formation of MC-130P Combat Shadows refuelled the ten helicopters. Despite the success of the mission, no WMDs were found at the palace.

Daily tactical reconnaissance missions continued throughout the air campaign, including sorties by the RQ-1 Predator and RQ-4 Global Hawk UAVs as well as by RAF Tornado GR4s equipped with the RAPTOR pod and F-14 Tomcats with the TARPS pod. On 3 April the Super Hornet Fast Tactical Imagery pod was used over Iraq for the first time by F/A-18Fs operating from USS *Abraham Lincoln*. The imagery from these sorties, fused with data from U-2S Dragon Lady, E-8 JSTARS and RC-135V/W Rivet Joint as well as

The crew of a USN EP-3E Aries II ISTAR platform ready for flight on 2 April 2003. The naval ISTAR aircraft of VQ-2 were placed under command of the 398th Air Expeditionary Group during the Iraq War. (NARA)

radar imagery from Onyx satellites was fed into the CAOC, both to identify targets for future tasking and to provide battle damage assessment to gauge the success of the strike missions already flown.

By 3 April, US ground forces were close to the outskirts of Baghdad. The focus of the air campaign was now on CAS tasking but the IQAF headquarters building at Muthanna airfield, which had been bombed previously was attacked again with JDAMs. F-15E Strike Eagles armed with 500lb GBU-12 LGBs ranged above the battlefield, knocking out individual tanks and AFVs. One pair of F-15Es operating in the Strike Coordination And Reconnaissance (SCAR) role, having delivered their own load of 9 GBU-12s, then acted as laser designators for following aircraft, marking for the delivery of a further 50 LGBs.

The fighting at the Haditha Dam continued through 3 April, albeit with slightly less activity than on previous days. A-10 Thunderbolts and RAF Harriers were called in once again. SOF Sgt Jeremy Feldbusch was severely wounded by an artillery strike and a rescue mission was initiated to evacuate him for medical attention. A force comprising an MH-47E Chinook escorted by two MH-60L Black Hawk DAPs flew in broad daylight, reaching the dam within an hour of the incident. Landing between artillery bombardments, the helicopters successfully recovered Feldbusch.

Saddam International Airport on the western outskirts of Baghdad was captured by V Corps on 4 April. The coalition used its overwhelming air power to crush any attempted counterattacks by Iraqi forces. Meanwhile, 1 MARDIV was advancing towards the eastern suburbs of the city, having destroyed the remnants of the Baghdad and Al Nida Divisions of the Republican Guard between Al Kut and Baghdad. A-10 Thunderbolts and attack helicopters were able to operate over the city and tankers and E-8 JSTARS were able to move their orbits further northwards to be closer to the battlefield.

The day also saw the establishment of a permanent detachment of A-10 Thunderbolts at Tallil. Basing the aircraft forward and thus reducing their transit time to their area of responsibility reduced the overall requirement for AAR considerably, easing the burden for the tanker force. It also meant that the A-10s could reach the front lines, now running just south of Baghdad, more quickly and could remain on station for a longer time. RAF Harriers were tasked into kill-boxes near Al Amarah, where they bombed military vehicles sheltering between defensive berms.

Among the 700 attack missions flown on 4 April was an attempt to kill Gen Ali Hassan al-Majid, a cousin of Saddam Hussein otherwise known as 'Chemical Ali' after he authorized the use of chemical weapons against Kurdish rebels in 1988. At 0530hrs two US aircraft dropped LGBs on a house in Basra which was allegedly owned by al-Majid, but it was later determined that he was not in the building at the time. Tornado GR4 tasking on the day included a three-missile Storm Shadow attack by two aircraft on a cable switching bunker at Kirkuk airfield and a signals intelligence facility in Baghdad. The Storm Shadows were launched from a position over the western desert. In the north of Iraq, Coalition aircraft engaged Iraqi forces near Kirkuk. In the western desert, the battle at the Haditha Dam continued and F-16s flew in support of the SOF team.

Australian Hornet strike

In the mid-morning of 5 April 2003, two RAAF F/A-18A Hornets flown by Sqn Ldr Terry van Haren (Executive Officer of 75 Squadron) and Flt Lt Anthony Dellasandro were tasked to conduct strikes against the infrastructure on the Rashid Airfield east of Baghdad. The site was thought to be a possible location of escape for the Iraqi leadership. This image depicts Sqn Ldr van Haren pulling up after releasing his weapons against a terminal building to the north of the main runway, which had been marked by a USAF A-10 with white phosphorous. Previous strikes by RAAF Hornets had destroyed a light transport aircraft on the taxiways.

Tallil airbase was opened for USAF operations from 31 March, thanks to the efforts of Lt Col Dave Kennedy and his team. These A-10 Thunderbolts are using the runway as a forward rearming and refuelling base during a mission on 3 April 2003. (NARA)

During their advance from Al Kut, 1 MARDIV had encountered foreign volunteers fighting for the Iraqi cause in the vicinity of Aziziyah, on the Tigris River roughly halfway between Al Kut and Baghdad. These paramilitary fighters were more tenacious than the Iraqi equivalents and fighting continued over the next days. During one engagement in the early hours of 5 April, three AH-1W SuperCobras gave support to a USMC unit that was under attack. As it manoeuvred to engage the enemy, one helicopter struck a communication mast with its rotor and crashed. The crew, Capts Travis A Ford and Benjamin W Sammis were killed. The incident served to illustrate the hazards of operating at low-level in the dark with NVGs under combat conditions. During the mid-morning, while F-15E Strike Eagles and F-16s prosecuted targets around western and northern Baghdad, RAAF F/A-18 Hornets attacked the Al Rashid airbase in the south-eastern outskirts of Baghdad. Intelligence sources indicated that it might be used as an avenue of escape for the Iraqi leadership. The first pair destroyed a transport aircraft on the taxiway and the second pair, comprising Sqn Ldr Terry van Haren and Flt Lt Anthony Dellasandro, bombed the terminal buildings and associated infrastructure with GBU-12 LGBs, after the target was marked by an A-10 AFAC with a white phosphorous rocket. USMC fixed-wing aircraft were also tasked with strikes later against the Abu Hayyah barracks in the north of Basra and a military camp at Al Amarah. These missions were as part of a larger package with USN and RAF aircraft, including Tornado GR4s, which struck three targets in the Abu Hayyah barracks. Later the USMC aircraft conducted another coordinated strike near Al Amarah in conjunction with a B-52 Stratofortress. A pair of A-10 Thunderbolts flown by Lt Col Richard D Turner and Lt Kim Campbell were tasked to destroy an abandoned SA-2 site to the north of Baghdad where they destroyed a divisional headquarters building with Mk82 bombs and strafed two transporters carrying a tank and SAM launcher. In the west, Harrier GR7s carried out two FAC-directed attacks in support of the TF20 team on the Haditha Dam. They destroyed two buildings which were being used as firing positions by Iraqi troops.

A HH-60G Pave Hawk Special Operations helicopter of the USAF Forces preparing to refuel from a KC-130 Hercules tanker aircraft during OIF on 6 April 2003. Extensive use was made of AAR to increase the range of the helicopters supporting SOF operations. (NARA)

During 6 April a mixed force of US SOF Teams and Kurdish *peshmerga* militia were engaged in a fierce fight with a larger and well-equipped Iraqi army force at the Debecka (Dibaga) crossroads 25mi south of Erbil. USN aircraft from the carriers in the Mediterranean were called in to provide CAS. F/A-18 Hornets, F-14D Tomcats and also USAF B-52 Stratofortresses knocked out at least eight Iraqi T-55 tanks and 16 APCs. Unfortunately, during one pass a Tomcat bombed *peshmerga* positions in error, causing a number of casualties.

Through the day A-10 Thunderbolts made good use of Tallil, with some aircraft based there semi-permanently and others cycling through to re-arm and refuel between sorties. In the afternoon, one pair of A-10 Thunderbolts flying from Tallil on their second sortie of the day was supporting 3rd Inf Div near Baghdad when, despite the poor visibility, the lead pilot Lt Col Raymond T Strasburger, noticed tanks and AFVs engaging the lightly armoured lead company. The Iraqi forces were positioned east of a bridge over the River Tigris and Lt Col Strasburger and his wingman Capt Gregory Thornton braved heavy AAA fire to investigate further. Despite having given up the element of surprise, the two A-10s carried out continuous attacks on the Iraqi forces for the next 30 minutes, killing three T-72 tanks, six APCs and many support vehicles. They left the area at dusk and still had to land on the

The battle for Baghdad

On the afternoon of 6 April 2003, A-10 pilots Lt Col Raymond 'Donk' Strasburger and Capt Gregory 'Billy Bob' Thornton carried out close air support for a force from US Task Force 269, 3rd Infantry Division at the Al Muthanna Bridge over the Tigris River in north-west Baghdad. The Forward Air Controller was Lt John 'Coke' Blocher. The image depicts Thornton firing his A-10's cannon at Iraqi T-72s on the circular traffic island to the east of the bridge. The attack was carried out under heavy anti-aircraft fire, which Strasburger described as puffs like popcorn around him. Previously hit targets around the eastern end of the bridge were also burning with black smoke.

airstrip at Tallil in darkness with blowing sand restricting the visibility. Troops from the 101st Airborne Div began clearing Iraqi paramilitary forces from Karbala. They were supported by F/A-18C Hornets firing laser guided AGM-65E Maverick missiles, as well as JDAM strikes.

While the priority for Coalition air power was the support of the land battles around Baghdad, the city of Tikrit, the original home of Saddam Hussein, began to be targeted. Three Tornado GR4 missions were flown against targets in and around Tikrit, including a FROG-7 missile storage facility and the runway at Tikrit airport, as well as a barracks in Ad Dawr, 10mi south of Tikrit. In some attacks the EPW II bombs were delivered using GPS guidance mode since the area was covered in cloud. Early in the morning of 7 April, F-15E Strike Eagles were in action, supporting SOF operations near Tikrit. At 0330hrs, one aircraft flown by Capt Eric B Das and Maj William R Watkins did not recover from a weapon delivery pass and flew into the ground. A rescue operation was immediately mounted to rescue the crew and a KC-135 Stratotanker crewed by Maj Brian Neitz, Capts Nathan Howard and Tricia Paulsen-Howe, and Tech Sgt Jim Pittman was directed to support this new mission. Despite being in a hostile area where AAA fire was still evident, the tanker crew established a refuelling orbit near Tikrit in order to give the search and rescue aircraft the maximum time in the search area. Unfortunately, however, an extensive search for the crew members of the Strike Eagle was unsuccessful and it became apparent that both of them had been killed in the crash.

On the same morning, Harrier GR7s provided overwatch as US Rangers deployed armoured vehicles that had been flown into H-1 airfield the previous night to relieve the team on the Haditha Dam. Approaching the dam, one Harrier was fired on by an SA-9 which the pilot was able to escape using flares and manoeuvre. On reporting the incident to the armoured convoy, the SA-9 vehicle was engaged and destroyed by the armoured vehicles, which then destroyed another five SA-9 vehicles. At this stage F-16s arrived to take over responsibility for covering the Coalition forces on and around the dam. Meanwhile A-10s and F-16s were also employed supporting the continuing SOF operations around Al Qa'im.

A F-14D Tomcat over skies of Iraq. Some of these aircraft were shore-based during the Iraq War, flying from Al Udeid airbase. (NARA)

Throughout the day, A-10 Thunderbolts were present overhead the Baghdad area, ready to respond to any requests for CAS. In the north-west of the city, a Republican Guard unit attempted to break out of the city at dawn to re-establish a corridor for reinforcements. However, it was blocked by units from 3rd Inf Div, supported by A-10s. During one such mission attacking a Republican Guard unit, the A-10 Thunderbolt flown by Capt Kim Campbell was hit by a MANPAD SAM which took out the hydraulic systems of the aircraft. Despite the catastrophic damage to the aeroplane, Campbell was able to recover safely to Al Jaber airbase. At the same time as the Iraqis attempted to drive out to the north-west, 3rd Inf Div mounted a 'Thunder Run' high speed dash with armour into central Baghdad. The tanks were supported by low-flying A-10 Thunderbolts and AH-64 Apaches and were able to fill the vacuum left by the Republican Guard and to seize control of the centre of the city. Meanwhile, 1 MARDIV had reached the south-eastern suburbs. As the Marines prepared to cross a bridge over the Diyala River, radio intercepts indicated that the Iraqi army were about to destroy the bridge with an artillery barrage. Air support was called in, in the shape of an EA-6B Prowler which used its electronic jamming capabilities to disrupt the Iraqi communications preventing the artillery from firing on the bridge. For urban CAS missions, the USMC flew in four-ship formations of two AH-1W SuperCobras, followed by two UH-1 Hueys which covered the rear hemisphere of the attack helicopters. Operating at low-level over the city, helicopters were frequently hit by ground fire and during the course of operations over Baghdad some 40 per cent of the Apaches sustained battle damage.

With the emphasis on CAS in an urban environment, some aircraft were loaded with inert (concrete) bombs in order to minimize collateral damage. However, the experiment was not entirely successful: when one flight of Tornado GR4s delivered inert EPW bombs accurately against a building under FAC direction, the FAC was dissatisfied with the results and called in a second strike using conventional high explosive weapons. During the day Coalition aircraft,

The typical weapon load of an F-16C during OIF included AIM-120 Advanced Medium Range Air-to-Air Missiles (AMRAAM), CBU-87 Combined Effects Munitions and Mark 84 2,000lb general purpose bombs. (NARA)

including Harrier GR7s, also continued to strike Iraqi forces around Al Amarah in support of TF Tarawa which was conducting clearing operations in the area.

Early in the afternoon, intelligence was received that Saddam Hussein was at a location in the Al Mansour district of Baghdad. A B-1B Lancer flown by Capts Chris Wachter and Sloan Hollis, Lt Col Fred Swan and 1st Lt Joe Runci, WSO had just completed AAR and was awaiting tasking when it was directed to bomb the building. At 1400hrs, just 47 minutes from receiving the intelligence input (and 12 minutes after the task had been passed to the B-1B crew) four 2,000lb GBU-31 JDAMs struck the target. The first GBU-31s were hard target penetrators and the second pair were set with 25msec. delay fuses to follow the penetrators into the same hole. However, it appears that Saddam had left the building shortly before the bomb strike, thus surviving another 'decapitation strike'.

A-10 Thunderbolts continued to operate at low-level around Baghdad on 8 April, but it was still a very dangerous environment, as two pilots discovered. At 1015hrs, the A-10 flown by Maj Jim Ewald was hit by a SAM, possibly a Roland, as he was completing a CAS sortie near Baghdad International airport. Ewald managed to fly clear of the city but after ten minutes he was forced to eject. He was quickly picked up by US troops. Maj Gary Wolf was more fortunate when his A-10 was hit by a SAM while carrying out a convoy overwatch. Although the missile destroyed the right engine, Wolf was able to fly the aircraft to Tallil airbase, where he made a safe landing. During the day, three quarters of the Coalition air component attack effort (a total of some 550 sorties) was dedicated to CAS.

As the focus of the ground campaign began to move to the north of Baghdad, the airlift of equipment and supplies into Bashur airbase continued. On 8 April C-17 Globemasters delivered five M1A1 Abrams tanks, five M2 Bradley fighting vehicles, 15 M113 APCs and 41 HMMWVs into Bashur. Another forward operating base was set up by the USMC to resupply 1 MARDIV before the final push into Baghdad. Marines secured the airstrip at Salman Pak on 8 April, establishing it as a base initially for two UH-1 Hueys, four AH-1W SuperCobras, four CH-53 Super Stallions, and two CH-46 Sea Knights. That night an almost continuous stream of KC-130 Hercules delivered fuel, ammunition and

The F/A-18 Hornet was the most numerous tactical aircraft deployed for OIF. This F/A-18C of the US Navy is armed with AIM-9 Sidewinder missiles, GBU-12 Paveway II 500lb laser guided bombs, and AGM-154A Joint Standoff Weapons (JSOW). (NARA)

rations into the airstrip. The runway was so narrow that the aircraft were unable to turn on it, so the KC-130 would land and then use reverse pitch to back the aeroplane along the runway to return to the active threshold for take-off. On the same evening just after dark, an MC-130H Combat Talon was the first Coalition aircraft to land at Baghdad (formerly Saddam) International Airport.

Organized Iraqi defences in Baghdad finally collapsed on 9 April as V Corps and 1 MARDIV troops pushed into the city. However, Coalition troops did still meet pockets of resistance. A-10 pilots Lt Col David T Kennedy and Maj William S Cuel were called in to provide emergency CAS for a USMC unit that was pinned down by a mixed force of Iraqi army and irregular soldiers. Both sides were in very close proximity, but the A-10 pilots carried out a low pass to visually separate them before strafing the Iraqi positions and breaking up the Iraqi assault. During the day, Coalition aircraft also bombed a building owned by Barzan Ibrahim Hasan al-Tikriti, a presidential adviser and half-brother of Saddam Hussein. The building in Ar Ramadi was razed by a strike with six JDAMs. Further south, having taken control of Basra, British forces advanced northwards to join up with TF Tarawa at Al Amarah.

On 10 April, Clearing operations continued in Baghdad while the newly constituted TF Tripoli, formed from elements of 1 MARDIV, advanced north towards Tikrit, where the last remnants of organized resistance were still holding out. These included the much-depleted Adnan Division of the Republican Guard and the Special Republican Guard. Of the 1,750 sorties flown on the day by Coalition aircraft, approximately one third were attack sorties, one quarter were airlift sorties and the remainder were AAR or intelligence gathering sorties. In the western desert F-16s supported the SOF operations around Al Qa'im. At one factory complex the workers had barricaded themselves into the premises and refused to surrender to Coalition troops. However, a supersonic low-level fly past by a pair of F-16s was enough to persuade them to change their minds.

RAF Tornado GR4s conducted a similar show of force at As Samawah the following day. Troops from V Corps were attempting to move civilians from a bridge and requested a low

An AH-64 Apache attack helicopter from the 2nd Battalion, 3rd Aviation Regiment, US Army blows up dust as it lands after a mission against surface-to-air threats near Baghdad on 11 April 2003. (NARA)

flypast to disperse the crowd. The Tornados flew two passes at 100ft and 600kts, which had the desired effect. However, the main focus of operations was further north. Two more Tornado GR4s were tasked by an RQ-1 Predator UAV to bomb a SAM radar near Tikrit. During the attack, the Predator laser designated the target, ensuring that the weapon dropped by the Tornado scored a direct hit. In another strike near Tikrit, at 1345hrs, a B-52 used a Litening II targeting pod for the first time, using it to laser designate a radar system at the airfield at Al Sahra, to the north-west of Tikrit. Harrier GR7s were also operating in the area during the day: a pair of Harriers bombed a military vehicle on the Al Sahra airfield and an S-60 AAA gun to the west of the airfield. In addition, Harrier GR7s flew CAS missions over the Haditha Dam, where an Iraqi tank was bombed, and over Al Qa'im.

While the Coalition ground forces advanced on Tikrit, clearing operations continued across Baghdad supported by CAS aircraft. On 11 April TF Tarawa moved into Tikrit, encountering little resistance, and the following day RAAF F/A-18 Hornets were tasked with overwatch as troops from the Australian SAS secured Al Asad airbase. This was the first time that RAAF aircraft had flown in direct support of Australian troops since the Vietnam War. Amongst other things, the Australian troops discovered 15 IQAF aircraft buried in the sand at the airbase. Although Al Asad was captured without a shot being fired, Iraq could still be a dangerous place for aircraft flying at low-level. A pair of MH-53M Pave Low helicopters were carrying out a combat resupply mission in darkness near Fallujah, when the lead aircraft was shot down by insurgents armed with rocket propelled grenades. In the Number 2 helicopter, Capt John M Groves managed to evade the hostile fire while making three attempts to land near his downed leader, eventually doing so and successfully rescuing the crew.

On 11 April, USMC AV-8B Harriers deployed to the repaired airfield at An Numaniyah, 25mi west of Al Kut. Operating from this forward location enabled the Harriers to spend longer on station while supporting USMC ground operations around Tikrit.

An MH-53M Pave Low IV helicopter from the 21st Special Operations Squadron, manoeuvres over a suspected hostile site in northern Iraq during a combat mission on 25 April 2003. The unit supported SOF operations throughout the Iraq War. (NARA)

Although there was no formal surrender by the Iraqi regime, it was clear that the campaign was coming to an end. Baghdad International Airport was fully under Coalition control by 13 April and on that day an RAAF C-130 Hercules flew in carrying medical supplies. The following day marked the end of major Coalition military operations in Iraq and the air campaign wound down accordingly. The last day that aircraft from all five USN carrier groups operated over Iraq was on 14 April, after which the two carrier battle groups led by USS *Constellation* and *Kitty Hawk* prepared to depart, leaving the USS *Nimitz*, *Harry S. Truman* and *Theodore Roosevelt* in the region. Coalition aircraft now concentrated on providing overwatch for the ground forces that were still involved in the clearing operations, and on supporting the humanitarian operation. The first humanitarian aid flight landed at Bashur on 16 April.

Over the next two weeks, the focus on the ground was in rooting out armed dissident groups and in re-establishing law and order in towns and cities where looting had become prevalent. From a daily total of 700 to 800 strike sorties, Coalition air forces were now typically flying only 100 to 200 daily strike sorties. By the end of the month the intensity of military operations had subsided sufficiently for President Bush to be able to declare that major combat operations had ended.

ANALYSIS

F/A-18 pilots from VFA-192 on the flight deck of USS *Kitty Hawk* after retuning from a successful mission over Iraq. (NARA)

By any measure, the invasion of Iraq was a great success. In just over three weeks the Iraqi regime had been overthrown and Coalition military forces controlled the country. The remarkably well-planned military operation was in some contrast to the post-conflict preparations and the Congressional Research Service reported to the US Congress in 2008 that 'most observers agree that the Administration's planning for "post-war" Iraq — for all the activities and resources that would be required on "the day after," to help bring about the strategic objective, a "free and prosperous Iraq" — was not nearly as thorough as the planning for combat operations'. However, the post-conflict planning and the conduct of military operations after the declaration of 'Mission Accomplished' by President Bush on 1 May 2003 lie outside the scope of this book.

Working together

Land, sea and air operations during the conflict itself demonstrated the effectiveness of well-equipped and well-trained military forces integrating together within a sound plan. In particular, the way in which the Coalition air forces worked together with each other and with Coalition land and sea forces illustrated the value of joint training. Lt Gen Moseley considered that 'the integrated Joint Coalition Plan – planning, execution, inclusion – worked better than anything that I have been involved in, at least in 40 years. Part of that is because we have all known each other. We have grown up in our own squadrons together; there are US guys in Australian squadrons, and Australian guys in US squadrons – same for the RAF. With NATO training standards we are all on the same template; we all understand this, we exchange with each other, "hostages" to each other's schools'. This perspective was echoed by AVM Glenn Torpy, the UK Air Contingent Commander, who said that 'everything I saw confirmed the collective and individual training that we had been undertaking for many years, much of it under a NATO banner. People can be disparaging about NATO but the one thing it delivered was standardization of equipment and our training outputs. In addition,

The targeting for Coalition aircraft during the Iraq War was led by intelligence and the diverse ISTAR spectrum, including the E-8C JOINT STARS (Joint Surveillance Target Attack Radar System). (NARA)

we had been flying with the US for 12 years in the No-Fly Zones. Many of us had grown up together, from being young fighter pilots to rather more mature colonels! That brought a level of trust and shared understanding that is probably unique to the RAF and USAF.'

The culture of co-operation and integration undoubtedly came from the top: Gen Franks was insistent on ground and air forces working together right from the initial planning phase and this was carried through by Lt Gen Moseley, who treated AVM Torpy and Gp Capt Geoff Brown, the RAAF contingent commander, as equal partners. The inclusion of Maj Gen Leaf into the Land Force component headquarters also ensured that lines of communication between the land and air components were kept open. That Moseley and Admiral Keating worked well together, and that Moseley managed to accommodate the demands of the USMC within his plans emphasizes how important it is for senior commanders to build cross-cultural partnerships rather than being dogmatically single service in their outlook.

One complication of the Coalition, which would also become apparent later during operations over Afghanistan, was the setting of differing Rules of Engagement (RoE) by the different nations involved. In some cases, the RoE set by the British and Australian governments were more restrictive than those applied to US forces, which meant that aircraft from those countries were unable to engage some targets, particularly those where there was a possibility of collateral damage. In future multi-national operations, the RoE for each national force would need to be streamlined.

Achievements of air power

At the start of the campaign, the Combined Force Air Component was given five tasks:
- The neutralization of the Iraqi command and control structure
- The suppression of Iraqi WMD including support of Coalition SOF
- The establishment of air supremacy over Iraq
- The support of Coalition land forces, including degrading the combat capability of Iraqi Army and Republican Guard forces before they could be engaged by Coalition land forces
- The support of Coalition maritime forces in the Persian Gulf

The neutralization of the Iraqi high-level command and communication structure was successfully achieved by the combined efforts of stealth technology F-117A Nighthawks and B-2A Spirits, B-1 Lancer and B-52 Stratofortress strategic bombers, tactical interdictor aircraft and naval TLAMs. The targeting was led by intelligence and the diverse ISTAR spectrum, ranging from satellites through reconnaissance aircraft to targeting pods carried on tactical aircraft. However, as AVM Torpy pointed out 'we [were] able to "hoover up" immense amounts of information, and improvements in sensor technology will only increase this capability. The challenge we face, however, is making sense of this huge amount of data so that it informs the campaign plan as it unfolds'. Another weakness of the Coalition intelligence network was the sparsity of reliable human intelligence (HUMINT) on the ground in Iraq, which meant that not all targets in regime occupied areas were correctly identified. For example, the two 'decapitation' attempts on Saddam Hussein on 20 March and 7 April were unsuccessful, but they did show how effectively the execution cycle for Time Sensitive Targets had been reduced to a matter of minutes. From late March, the destruction of the command-and-control structure meant that the Iraqi army was unable to function as a cohesive fighting force, leaving individual units to be picked off by air power before they could join the battle.

The counter-TBM campaign in the western desert was also highly successful. Thanks to their specialized training before the conflict, the Coalition air units were able to integrate seamlessly into the SOF ground operations. As one RAF Harrier pilot expressed it at the end of the war 'we put so much effort into finding the missiles that we created the effect desired and scared them off'. Once again, the input of the various specialist reconnaissance assets was invaluable. The work of the Special Operations transport aircraft, both fixed-wing and helicopter, was also crucial to inserting, extracting and re-supplying the SOF teams.

Air supremacy over Iraq was established relatively quickly, by 7 April, mainly thanks to the earlier Operation *Southern Focus* which had started the work of dismantling the Iraqi air defences from June 2002. Lt Gen Moseley explained that 'we [had] conducted a fairly aggressive campaign called *Southern Focus*. Every time we would get shot at by a 57 mm,

During the Iraq War, B-2 Spirits were armed with precision guided weapons such as JDAM and JSOW. This B-2 is seen during a combat mission on 27 March 2003. (NARA)

which was a lot, or even radar-guided 85 mm or the mobile SAMs, we would respond with attacks on command-and-control bunkers, on fibre-optic cables and nodes, and on the gun pits themselves. By the time we got to H-hour, we did not need three days or four days or five days; everything south of Baghdad was pretty much gone… I think that most people who look at the Iraqi campaign perhaps have not focused on what *Southern Focus* really meant. What it really provided was an effect prior to H-hour'. The no-show of the IQAF was doubtless due to the intimidation of the Iraqi high command by the overwhelmingly superior force ranged against them: Coalition fighter pilots were doubtless frustrated at their lack of trade, but they had achieved their aim by their mere presence. The SAM defences presented more of a challenge, but the radars were systematically taken down by HARM-shooting F-16CJ, EA-6B Prowlers and F/A-18 Hornets, and the missile launchers and support systems were bombed by tactical aircraft as well as B-2 Spirits with precision-guided weapons such as JDAM and JSOW. AAA guns were targeted in a similar way. The individual elements of the Iraqi mobile SAM/AAA order of battle were located by U-2 and Global Hawk, enabling them to be targeted efficiently.

The major effort of the air component was in supporting the land battle and once again it can be judged as a complete success. In its assessment of the campaign, the US Army Operation *Iraqi Freedom* Study Group recorded that 'on more than one occasion, responsive accurate close air support turned the tide for Army ground troops… Time and time again during OIF, airmen intervened at critical points on the battlefield'. Nevertheless, as Lt Gen Moseley commented there were still 'problems with battlespace deconfliction. Pushing the fire support coordination line beyond the SAMs is not a good thing. We had problems with air defence and the Patriot missile system… Some of my Marine brothers still believed that they were going to conduct a completely separate air effort, because that is what they normally do doctrinally. We went through that a little bit and we got that worked out'. But in the event, 1 MEF was more successful than the US Army in tasking and utilizing

The scene aboard an EC-130J Command Solo psychological warfare aircraft during an Operation *Southern Focus* mission on 6 March 2003. In preparation for the coming conflict, television and radio programming was broadcast directly into Iraq, telling military personnel how they could surrender to Coalition forces. (NARA)

air support. The USMC DASC concept proved far more responsive and flexible than the Army ASOC and from an early stage of the war aircrew expressed a strong preference to be tasked into the 1 MEF Area Of Responsibility (AOR), rather than the V Corps AOR; many aircraft tasked to support the US Army ended up returning to base with their weapons on board because the ASOC could not find them targets. The extended FSCL in the Army AOR also reduced the efficiency of air interdiction in shaping the battlespace ahead of the advancing ground forces. As the official UK government First Reflections document stated, 'the operation also highlighted that the integration of Close Air Support aircraft requires further refinement and practice'. However, despite these difficulties, Coalition air power was remarkably effective in destroying both the equipment and the will to fight of the Iraqi forces. Reduced to sending its units piecemeal towards the battlefield, the Republican Guard found itself being decimated by sustained air attack. Even the *shamal* that had halted the Coalition advance offered no sanctuary to the Iraqi land forces. The attrition of the Iraqi Army and Republican Guard by air attack greatly reduced the size, strength and fighting capacity of forces resisting the Coalition advance.

Two more areas of friction in the integration of Army and Air Component operations were the use of the AH-64 Apache and the fratricide by Army Patriot SAM systems. The ill-fated long-range strike by the 11th Aviation Regiment illustrated the need to use the right weapon system to achieve a task. A long-range interdiction mission should properly have been the responsibility of fixed-wing interdictor aircraft, such as the F-15E Strike Eagle or Tornado GR4, rather than an attack helicopter which is extremely well-suited to the CAS mission, but less so to long-range roles. In attempting to duplicate interdiction efforts, the Apache regiment almost sealed its own fate and even the apparently more successful subsequent mission produced pitiful results. The episode seems to indicate an unhelpful inter-service rivalry rather than a desire to achieve a result in the most efficient manner. A similar unwillingness to work to a joint – rather than single service – plan resulted in

Undoubtedly the most critical element of the air campaign was the provision of air-to-air refuelling. Here a USAF KC-135R Stratotanker refuels a US Navy F/A-18 Hornet during a mission on 11 April 2003. The Coalition AAR fleet included the KC-10A Extender as well as RAF VC-10 and TriStars and USN types such as the S-3B Viking and F/A-18E/F Super Hornet. (NARA)

The routine use of PGMs increased the combat efficiency of air power. These are GBU-31A 1,000lb satellite-guided Joint Direct Attack Munitions (JDAM) at Al Udeid in early April 2003. The RAF also used satellite-guided PGMs in the shape of the 1,000lb Enhanced Paveway II. (NARA)

the unnecessary deaths of three Coalition aircrew in blue-on-blue incidents by Patriot SAM batteries and a near miss on another occasion. These were unforgivable lapses by the Patriot crews.

Tactical transport operations in support of ground forces, and in particular as part of the SOF operations in northern Iraq were another success story. The infiltration of the SOF teams into Bashur and the subsequent combat jump by the 173rd Airborne Brigade were testament to the professionalism of the aircrews involved.

With the emphasis on the land campaign inside Iraq, support of Coalition maritime operations was, in comparison, a relatively minor task. However, it was still an important one, which was carried out successfully in the main by Coalition MPA such as the P-3C Orion and Nimrod MR2 as well as carrier-borne aircraft. Even so, many of these aircraft were diverted to a new role as ISTAR platforms.

Perhaps the most critical element of the whole air campaign was the provision of AAR. With few exceptions, most of the aircraft operating over Iraq were dependent on AAR to achieve their tasks. AAR enabled strategic aircraft like the B-2A Spirit and B-52 Stratofortress to operate over Iraq from distant bases such as Diego Garcia, Fairford in the UK and Whiteman airbase in Missouri USA. The same is true on a smaller scale for the tactical aircraft operating from airbases, and aircraft carriers, outside the boundaries of Iraq. In addition, AAR enabled aircraft to remain on station over Iraq for extended periods, thus maximizing their combat effectiveness. The differing techniques (boom-and-receptacle versus probe-and-drogue) used on the one hand by the USAF and on the other by the USN, USMC, RAF and RAAF complicated the issue of tanker allocation, as did the denial of Saudi and Turkish airspace for the AAR support of offensive missions. As a result of the latter restrictions, tanker aircraft were based at airfields as far away as Moron airbase in Spain, Burgas in Bulgaria, Akrotiri in Cyprus and Cairo West in Egypt. The relatively small number of tanker aircraft in comparison to the Gulf War 12 years previously meant that the demand for tankers exceeded the provision. This shortage of AAR capacity particularly affected USN carrier-borne aircraft. Vice Adm Keating considered that 'the tanker issue has sparked a lot of controversy. The differences between Desert Storm and this operation were significant. In Desert Storm, we had 346 tankers at five bases, the best tanker bases in the world. They were all filled with large pipelines to sustain those tankers. At the start of this war, we only had 160 tankers at 15 bases and the infrastructure to feed them was by trucks. So we eventually ramped up to 200 tankers. Everybody asked, "Where are all the tankers?" Quite frankly, there was a dramatic difference from how we remembered it in the past to the challenges that confronted us here. And that's the tanker story that people tend to forget. It was basing and infrastructure to feed the tankers that drove the air war, and we had to apportion appropriately'. Imaginative use of the S-3 Viking and F/A-18E/F Super Hornet as tanker aircraft ameliorated the problem for the Navy to some extent. For the USAF and USMC, the solution was to forward-base tactical aircraft on bases within Iraq such as Tallil and An Numaniyah. Nevertheless, despite the challenges, the tanker-to-total-sortie ratio during the Iraq War was twice that achieved during the Gulf War: during the conflict Coalition tankers refuelled over 29,000 receivers during 9,064 sorties.

Efficiencies

Benefitting from an open culture of joint operations, full manning and prior operational experience over both Iraq and Afghanistan, the CAOC functioned with great efficiency during the Iraq war. During the Gulf War it had taken 14 hours to plan and execute 3,000 sorties, but in 2003 the time had been reduced just six hours. The whole planning cycle had been reduced, making air power more responsive to the situation on the ground. Multiple ISTAR inputs giving real-time feedback also ensured that air assets were employed efficiently.

The routine use of PGMs also increased the combat efficiency of air power. During the Iraq War, Coalition aircraft delivered a total of 19,948 PGMs and 9,251 unguided weapons,

UAVs, including the RQ-4 Global Hawk shown here, were invaluable for their ability to loiter over the battlefield for extended periods. Other UAVs, such as the R/MQ-1 Predator, were able to locate and laser designate targets for Coalition aircraft to attack. (US DoD)

a usage rate of PGMs of 68 per cent; in the Gulf War the percentage of PGMs had been just eight per cent of the total weapon expenditure. The use of PGMs gave the Coalition the means of attacking point targets selectively with deadly accuracy and of striking enemy forces even when the weather conditions would have offered sanctuary in the past. It also reduced the amount of collateral damage that was caused, thereby minimizing the risk of civilian hostility towards the Coalition.

UAVs proved their worth during the Iraq War both as reconnaissance platforms and as strike aircraft. The RQ-4 Global Hawk was invaluable for its ability to loiter for up to 34 hours over the AOR and, amongst other tasks, to carry out pre-strike checks of kill-boxes to update strike aircraft with target positions or advise if the kill-box was empty. Similarly, the RQ-1/MQ-1 demonstrated how UAVs could be used both as target finders for other aircraft and also as autonomous strike platforms. Although UAVs are expensive machines and should not therefore be exposed to undue risk, they give the ability to fly an aircraft in a hostile environment which might be considered too risky for a manned aeroplane. Thus, UAVs increase yet further the reach and efficiency of air power.

CONCLUSION

The air campaign over Iraq in 2003 was probably the first true joint services operation in which air operations were completely integrated with the land campaign. The 41,404 sorties flown by Coalition aircraft during the hostilities formed an integral part of the overall land/air battle and shaped the battlefield to give Coalition land forces the very best prospects of success. Sound planning and intelligent, and intelligence-led, use of modern technology ranging from computer-based mission planning, through reconnaissance sensors and UAVs, to satellite-guided munitions ensured that air power was able to fulfil the critical roles allotted to it. Many of the positive lessons learnt over Iraq, particularly in joint service and multi-national operations, shaped the prosecution of the subsequent counter-insurgency operations over Iraq after the cessation of formal hostilities as well as the air campaign over Afghanistan. Overall, the air campaign over Iraq in March and April 2003 was an unqualified success.

A post-conflict flypast by representatives of the tactical combat aircraft which participated in the Iraq War. Behind a KC-135 tanker, from top to bottom: Tornado GR4 (RAF), F-16CJ, F-15E, F-117, F-15E, F-16CJ, F/A-18A (RAAF). (USAF)

FURTHER READING

There are, as yet, relatively few books about the air war over Iraq in 2003. However, *The Unseen War – Allied Air Power and the Takedown of Saddam Hussein*, Benjamin S Lambeth (Naval Institute Press, 2013) gives a good high-level overview of the campaign, including the views of the commanders. The Center for Strategic and International Studies published *The Lessons of the Iraq War: Main Report*, Anthony H Cordeman (CSIS, 2003) which also gives details and an assessment of the campaign.

For a fuller overall picture of the conflicts in Iraq since the start of the 1991 Gulf War, *Cradle of Conflict – Iraq and the Birth of the Modern US Military*, Michael Knights (Naval Institute Press, 2005) is an excellent account of Coalition military involvement in Iraq from 1991 through to the aftermath of the Iraq War. At an operational level, *Flying in the Face of Fear – A Fighter Pilot's Lessons on Leading With Courage*, Kim 'KC' Campbell (John Wiley & Sons, 2023) offers the perspective of an A-10 pilot who flew during the Iraq War. *The RAF in Operation Telic*, Sebastian Ritchie (UK MOD, 2023) is the official history of the RAF involvement in the Iraq War.

A good amount of detail about air operations in support of SOF operations can be found in the *Air Commando Journal*, Vol 2 Issue 4 and Vol 9 Issue 2 which can be downloaded from the Air Commando Association website www.aircommando.org. Further descriptions of the participation of specific aircraft types in the conflict can be found in the following titles within the Osprey 'Combat Aircraft' series: *US Navy Hornet Units of Operation Iraqi Freedom (Part One)* (COM 46), *F-15C/E Eagle Units of operation Iraqi Freedom* (COM 47), *US Navy F-14 Tomcat Units of Operation Iraqi Freedom* (COM 52), *US Marine Corps and RAAF Hornet Units of Operation Iraqi Freedom* (COM 56), *US Navy Hornet Units of Operation Iraqi Freedom (Part Two)* (COM 58), *B-1B Lancer Units in Combat* (COM 60), *F-16 Fighting Falcon Units of Operation Iraqi Freedom* (COM 61), *AV-8B Harrier II Units of Operation Iraqi Freedom I-VI* (COM 99), *RAF Tornado Units in Combat 1992–2019* (COM 142), *Harrier GR7/9 Units in Combat* (COM 151).

SELECTED GLOSSARY

AAR	Air-to-Air Refuelling
AIM	Air Intercept Missile
ALARM	Air Launched Anti-Radiation Missile
ALIC	Avionics/Launcher Interface Computer
AMRAAM	Advanced Medium Range Air-To-Air Missile
ASM	Air-to-Surface Missile
ASRAAM	Advanced Short Range Air-to-Air Missile
ATO	Air Tasking Order
AWACS	Airborne Warning And Control System
CALCM	Conventional Air Launched Cruise Missile
CAOC	Combined Air Operations Center
CAS	Close Air Support
CENTAF	US Central Command Air Forces
CENTCOM	The United States Central Command
CFACC	Combined Force Air Component Commander
CFLCC	Combined Forces Land Component Commander
CRAF	Civil Reserve Air Fleet
DAP	Direct Action Penetrator
FLIR	Forward Looking Infrared
HARM	High-Speed Anti-Radiation Missile
IOC	Intercept Operations Centers
ISTAR	Intelligence, Surveillance, Target Acquisition and Reconnaissance
JDAM	Joint Direct Attack Munition
JSTARS	Joint Surveillance Target Attack Radar System
LANTIRN	Low-Altitude Navigation and Targeting Infrared for Night
LGB	Laser Guided Bombs
MARDIV	Marine Division
MEF	Marine Expeditionary Force
MEZ	Missile Engagement Zone
MTI	Moving Target Indicator
NFZ	No-Fly Zone
NVG	Night Vision Goggles
OIF	Operation *Iraqi Freedom*
OPLAN	Operational Plan
OSW	Operation *Southern Watch*
PGM	Precision Guided Munitions
PSAB	Prince Sultan Air Base
PSYOP	Psychological Operations
RAF	(British) Royal Air Force
RAAF	Royal Australian Air Force
SAR	Synthetic Aperture Radar
SCUD	Soviet-made R-300 Tactical Ballistic Missile
SEAD	Suppression of Enemy Air Defence
SOC	Sector Operations Center
TADS/PNVS	Target Acquisition and Designation Sights/Pilot Night Vision System
TARPS	Tactical Air Reconnaissance Pod System
TBM	Tactical Ballistic Missile
TERCOM	Terrain Contour Matching
TFR	Terrain Following Radar
TIALD	Thermal Imaging Airborne Laser Designator
TLAM	Tomahawk Land Attack Missiles
TST	Time Sensitive Targets
UAV	Unmanned Air Vehicle
USCENTCOM (COMUSNAVCENT)	United States Central Command (Commander, U.S. Naval Forces Central Command)
USAF	United States Air Force
USMC	United States Marine Corps
USN	United States Navy
WMD	Weapons of Mass Destruction

INDEX

Figures in **bold** refer to illustrations.

Advanced Medium Range Air-To-Air Missile (AMRAAM) **13**, 15, 21, **44**, 49, **79**
Afghanistan 9–10, **13**, 15, 19, 24, 33, 85, 90, 92
Air Intercept Missile (AIM) **13**, 15, 21, **44**, 49, **79**, **80**
air-to-air refuelling (AAR) 15, 23, 37, **56**, 65, 70–71, **75**, 80–81, **88**, 89–90
 AAR tankers 15, 17–18, 20–21, 37, 42, 46, 53, 56, 64
Airborne Forward Air Controllers (AFAC) 20, 52, 61–63, 66, 74
Airborne Warning And Control System (AWACS) 15, 20–21, 46, 53, 62
aircraft:
 Bell:
  AH-1W SuperCobra 12, 20, 43, **45**, 52, 61, 63, 74, 79–80
  UH-1 Huey 20, 43, 52, 64, 79–80
 Boeing:
  AH-64 Apache 11, 22–23, 44, 52, 56–57, 62, 79, **81**, 88
  B-52 Stratofortress **16**, 17, 64, 66, 74–75, 86, 89
  C-17 Globemaster 11–12, 14, 23, 59–61, **69**, 80
  Chinook HC2: 20, 39, **40**, 49, **50**, 58, **60**, 65
  KC-135 Stratotanker 15, 37, 78, **88**, **92**
  RC-135V/W Rivet Joint 17, **23**, 52, 58, 70
 Boeing Vertol:
  CH-46 Sea Knight 11, 20, 43, 68, 80
 British Aerospace:
  Harrier GR7: 20–21, 36–38, **40**, 42–44, 46, 49, 52, 59, 61, 63, **64**, 65–66, 68–69, 71, 74, 78, 80, 82, 86
 English Electric:
  Canberra PR9: 20, 37, **39**, **40**, 61
 Fairchild:
  A-10 Thunderbolt 11–12, 16, 36–37, **40**, 42, 49, 52, 59–61, 63, **65**, 66, 68–70, **71**, **74**, **75**, 78–81
 General Atomics:
  MQ-1 Predator 11, 17, 48, **90**, 91
  RQ-1 Predator 17, 29, 39, 53, 61, 65, 70, 82
 General Dynamics:
  F-16 Fighting Falcon **15**, 16, **36**, 37, **40**, 42, 46, 52, 58, 65, 68, 71, 74, 78, **79**, 81
  F-16CJ Wild Weasel 11, **15**, 16, 34, 42, 44, **46**, 48, 57, **62**, 70, 87, **92**
 Grumman:
  EA-6B Prowler 18, 20, 34, **38**, 42, 44–45, 48, 60, 70, 79, 87

  F-14 Tomcat 12, 17–18, **40**, **53**, 69–70, 75, **78**
 Hawker Siddeley:
  Nimrod MR2: 20–21, 39, 52, 61, **68**, 89
 Lockheed:
  AC-130U Spooky 16, 36, 42–43, 52, 59, 66, 68
  C-130 Hercules 14, 20, **22**, **40**, 49, **50**, **54**, 60, 65, 70, 83
  F-117 Nighthawk 11, 16, 34, **39**, 42, 44, 48, 56, 86, **92**
  KC-130 Hercules 20, 53, 60, 66, **75**, 80–81
  MC-130H Combat Talon II 11–12, 17, **40**, 46, 49, **50**, **51**, **59**, 81
  P-3C Orion 18–19, **22**, 43, 52, 89
  S-3 Viking 12, 18, 37, 53, 56, 59, 68, **88**, 90
  U-2S Dragon Lady 17, **18**, **40**, 58, 69–70
 McDonnell Douglas:
  AV-8B Harrier 12, **19**, 20, 36, 52, **63**, 64–65, 68, 82
  F/A-18 Hornet **4**, **8**, 11–12, 18, 20–21, **22**, 36, **43**, 44, 49, 52, 56, **58**, 59, 61–62, **63**, 69, **71**, 74–75, 78, **80**, 82, **84**, 87, **88**, **92**
  F/A-18E/F Super Hornet 18, 37, 53, 64, 70, **88**, 90
  F-15 Eagle **6**, **14**, 15, 34, 46
  F-15E Strike Eagle 12, **13**, 15, 36, **40**, 42, **44**, 58, 61, 66, 68, 70–71, 74, 78, 88, **92**
 Northrop Grumman:
  B-2 Spirit 11, 16–17, 44, 48, 56, 61, 64, **86**, **87**, 89
  RQ-4 Global Hawk 17, 52, 70, 87, **90**, 91
 Panavia:
  Tornado F3: 20–21, 34, 46, **52**
  Tornado GR4: 11, 20, **21**, 34, 36, **40**, 43, 45, **48**, 49, **53**, 58, 61–63, 66, 70–71, 74, 78–79, 81–82, 88, **92**
 Rockwell:
  B-1B Lancer 11–12, 16–17, 34, 36, 38, 42, 48, 58–59, **61**, 64, 80, 86
 Sikorsky:
  MH-53M Pave Low 17, 23, **40**, 44–45, 67, 78, **82**
  MH-60 Black Hawk 12, 23, 39, 69–71
Al Amarah 11, **47**, 48, 61, 63, 71, 74, 80–81
airbases and airfields:
 Al Asad **27**, 28, 48, 65, 82
 Al Jaber **7**, 14, 16, **19**, 20, **63**, **64**, 79
 Al Udeid **7**, 13, **14**, 15–16, 18, 20, **21**, **22**, 39, 42, 45, 61, 63, 69, **78**, **89**
 Ali Al Salem **7**, 7, 11, 14, 20, **21**, 43, 45, **48**,

  49, 61, 63, 70
 Arar 39, **40**, 45, 49, **50**, 70
 Azraq **7**, 14, 16, 20, 61
 Bashur 11–12, **27**, 49, **51**, 59, 61, **67**, **69**, 80, 83, 89
 Diego Garcia **7**, 14, **16**, 17, 64, **66**, 89
 H-2: **27**, 43, 49, 61, 63
 H-3 (Al Walid) 26, **27**, 38, 42–43
 King Faisal **7**, 14, 20, 49, **50**
 Prince Sultan Air Base (PSAB) **7**, 13–14, **15**, 20–21, 42
 Sulaymaniyah 11, **27**, 49, **51**, **67**
 Tallil (Imam Ali) 11, 26, **27**, **44**, 49, 66, 71, **74**, 75, 78, 80, 90
Al Faw peninsula 11, 18, 23, 33, 39, 43
Al Kut 12, **47**, 52, 56, 61, 63, 68, 71, 74, 82
Al Qa'im **40**, 46, **67**, 78, 81–82
An Najaf 11, **47**, 49, 56–58, 60, 62–63, 66
An Nasiriyah 11–12, 26, **47**, 52, 59–60, 63, 65, 68
Anti-Aircraft Artillery (AAA) 6, 18, 25–26, 28–29, **30**, 38, 48–49, **51**, **53**, 56–57, 59, 75, 78, 82, 87

Ba'ath Party regime 4, 8, 10, 32, 42, 59, 61, 65–66
Baghdad 11–12, 19, 25, 26, **28**, 29, **31**, 32–34, 42, 44–46, **47**, 48–49, **53**, 56, 61, 63–64, 66, **67**, 68–70, **71**, 74, **75**, 78–80, **81**, 82, 87
Baghdad (previously Saddam) International Airport 12, **25**, 56, 64, 71, 80–81, 83
Basra 12, 28, 39, 42, **47**, 59–61, 63, 69, 71, 74, 81
Bush, President George W 4, **5**, 8–12, 30, 32, 38, 42, 83–84

Close Air Support (CAS) 12, 16, **19**, 22, 29, 31, **35**, 36–37, 42, 44, **45**, 46, 49, 52, 56–60, **61**, 62, **65**, 68, 71, **75**, 79–82, 87–88
Coalition forces **4**, 5–6, 8–13, 18, 20–26, 28–34, 36–39, 42–44, 46, 48–49, **52**, **56**, 57–58, 60, **61**, 63, **65**, 66, 68–69, 71, 78–84, **85**, 86, **87**, **88**, 89, **90**, 91–92
Combined Air Operations Center (CAOC) 13, **14**, 20, 24, 39, 42, 53, 58, 68–69, 71, 90

Direct Action Penetrator (DAP) 12, 23, 39, 69–71

Fire Support Coordination Line (FSCL) **35**, 36, 44, 49, 57, 87–88
Forward Air Controller (FAC) 20, 36–37, 52, 57, 59, 61, 69, 74, **75**, 79
Forward Arming and Refuel Point (FARP) 56–57, 60–62

Gulf War 4, 8, 10, 24, 26, 28, 33–34, **35**, 37, 45, 89–91

INDEX

Haditha Dam 12, **40**, 60, 63, 66, 69, 71, 74, 78, 82
Hellfire missiles 17, 20, 22, 39, 48, 57, 62
High-Speed Anti-Radiation Missile (HARM) 11, **15**, 16, 18, 34, 44, **46**, 57–58, 60, 87
Hussein, Saddam 4–5, 10–12, 25, **26**, 29–32, 38, 42, 70–71, 78, 80–81, 86

Intelligence, Surveillance, Target Acquisition and Reconnaissance (ISTAR) **18**, **23**, 24, 34, **68**, **70**, **85**, 86, 89–90
Intercept Operations Centers (IOC) 26, 38, 42, 45, 48
Iraq War 4, **14**, **18**, 19, **21**, 26, **28**, 29, **34**, **35**, **53**, **58**, **60**, **65**, **70**, **78**, **82**, **85**, **86**, 90–91, **92**
Iraqi Air Force (IQAF) 25, **28**, 29, 34, 38, 46, 49, **52**, 53, 71, 82, 87
Iraqi Army 10, 30–31, 33, 75, 79, 81, 85–86, 88
Israel 7, 32–33, **40**, 46, **50**

Joint Direct Attack Munition (JDAM) 11, **16**, 17–18, 21, 43, 48, 56, 58–59, **61**, 64, 69, 71, 78, 80–81, **86**, 87, 89
Joint Surveillance Target Attack Radar System (JSTARS) 17, 52, 58–59, 70–71, **85**
Jordan 7, 11, 14–15, 20, 26, **27**, 37–38, **39**, **40**, 42, 49, **50**, 69

Karbala 12, **47**, 61–63, 66, **67**, 68–69, 78
kill-boxes **34**, **35**, 36, 71, 91
Kirkuk 26, **27**, 28, 44–45, **53**, 58, 63, **67**, 71
Kuwait 4, 7, 11, 14, **19**, 20, **21**, 32–33, **36**, **40**, 42–44, **45**, **47**, 60, **63**, 64

Laser Guided Bombs (LGB) 12–13, 16, 18, **21**, 22, 24, **39**, 42, **44**, 45, 49, **58**, 61, 64–65, 69, 71, 74, 78–79, **80**, **89**
Litening II targeting pod **13**, 52, 65, 68, 82

Maritime Patrol Aircraft (MPA) 18, 20, **22**, 52, **68**, 89
Maverick missiles 16, 21, 44, 59, 69, 78
Mediterranean Sea 7, 17, 37, 49, 57–58, 66, 75
Moseley, Lt Gen T Michael 13, **14**, 20, 24, 32–34, 84–87

Night Vision Goggles (NVG) 17, 43, 49, **51**, **53**, 57, 59–60, 70, 74
No-Fly Zone (NFZ) 5, **6**, 8, 10, 13–14, 17, 20, 24, 26, 28–29, 34, 38, 85

operations:
 Iraqi Freedom (OIF) 4, 10, 13–16, 20, **23**, **33**, 34, 42, **56**, **58**, **59**, **61**, **75**, **79**, **80**, 87
 Southern Focus 8–9, 11, 34, 38, 86, **87**
 Southern Watch (OSW) 4, 5, **6**, 14–15, 38, 42

Persian Gulf 7, 10, 12, 17, **19**, 20–23, 33, 42, 44, 48, 58, 68, 85
peshmerga 12, 22, 37, 63, 75
Precision Guided Munitions (PGM) **16**, 24, **89**, 90–91

Qatar 7, 13, **14**, 15, **21**, **22**, **40**

radar 11, 15–19, 21–22, 25–26, 28–29, **38**, 39, 42, 44–46, 49, 52, **53**, 57, 60, 65, 71, 82, **85**, 87
Republican Guard 4, 11, 22, 25, 29–31, 33, 36, 42, 45, 48–49, 56, 58, 61–63, 65–66, 68, 71, 79, 81, 85, 88
rivers:
 Euphrates 10–11, 33, **47**, 49, 52, 58–59, 63, 66, **67**
 Tigris 10–12, 33, **47**, 61, 64, **67**, 68, 74, **75**
Royal Air Force (British) (RAF) 6, 11, 13, 17, 20, **21**, 24, 34, 36, **37**, 38, **39**, 42–44, **45**, 46, **48**, 49, **50**, **52**, 58–59, **60**, 61–63, **64**, 65, **68**, 69–71, 74, 81, 84–86, **88**, **89**, 92
Royal Australian Air Force (RAAF) 11, 13, 18, 21, **22**, 24, 49, 56, **58**, **71**, 74, 82–83, 85, 89, **92**
Royal Marine (British) (RM) 11, 19, 23, 43–44
Royal Navy (British) (RN) 11, 13, 23–24, 48

Saudi Arabia 7, 13, **14**, **15**, 26, **27**, 33, **40**, **45**, **47**, **50**
shamal 10–11, 57–58, **61**, **62**, **63**, 88
Special Operations Forces (SOF) 9–12, 17, 20, 22, 32–33, 37, 39, **40**, 42–43, 45–46, 49, **50**, 52, **59**, **60**, 61, 63, 65–66, **68**, 70–71, **75**, 78, 81, **82**, 85–86, 89
Storm Shadow missile 21, 34, 45, **48**, **53**, 61, 63, 71
Super Missile Engagement Zone (Super-MEZ) 19, 26, 28, 34, 44, 48
Suppression of Enemy Air Defence (SEAD) **15**, 16, 18, 21, 44–45, **46**, 48–49, 53, 56–57, 62
Surface-to-Air Missiles (SAM) 6, 11–12, 16, 18–19, 23, **25**, 26, 28–30, 38–39, 42, 44, 49, 53, 56, 58–60, **64**, 65–66, 68–70, 74, 79–80, **81**, 82, 87–89

Tactical Ballistic Missile (TBM) 10, 14, 20, 22–24, **26**, 30, **31**, 32–33, 37, **39**, **40**, **41**, 42–43, 46, 52, 60–61, **65**, 86
Task Forces (TF) 12, 19–20, 39, **40**, 43, **47**, 49, **50**, 52, 58–59, 63, 65–66, **67**, 69, 74, **75**, 80–82
Tikrit **9**, 12, 19, 25–26, 28, 34, 44, **67**, 78, 81–82
Tomahawk Land Attack Missiles (TLAM) 19, 24, 34, 42, 44, 46, 48, 56, 64, 86
Turkey 7, 9–10, 14–15, 20, **27**, 33, 37, **51**

United Kingdom (UK) 5, 9, 17, **37**, 44, 84, 88–89
United Nations (UN) 5–6, 9–10, 30
United States of America (USA) 4–5, 8–9, 14, 25, 89
United States (US) Army 11–13, 20, 22–23, **33**, 36, 42, 44, **47**, 49, 52, 57–58, 60, 68–69, **81**, 87–88
 3rd Infantry Division (3rd Inf Div) 11–12, 22, 33, 44, 49, 63, 66, 68, **75**, 79
 11th Aviation Regiment 11, 22, 56, 62, 88
 101st Airborne Division 11, 22, 33, **47**, 66, 78
 173rd Airborne Brigade 11, 23, 59, 66, **67**, 89
 V Corps 22, 33, 36, **47**, 49, 56, 63, 66, **67**, 68, 71, 81, 88
United States Air Force (USAF) **6**, 11–13, **14**, **15**, 16–18, 23–24, 34, **35**, **36**, 37, **44**, 46, 49, **50**, 52, 57, **59**, **69**, **71**, **74**, **75**, 85, **88**, 89–90, **92**
United States Central Command (CENTCOM / USCENTCOM) 6, 8, 13, 32, **33**, **34**, **35**
United States (US) Central Command Air Forces (CENTAF) 13–15, 18, 21
United States Marine Corps (USMC) 11–13, 18, **19**, 20–21, 24, 33, 36–37, 42, **43**, **45**, 52–53, 60–61, **63**, 64, 74, 79–82, 85, 88–90
 1st Marine Division (1 MARDIV) 11–12, 19, 52, 63, 66, 68, 71, 74, 79–81
 1st Marine Expeditionary Force (1 MEF) **19**, 20, 33, 36, **47**, 53, **67**, 68, 87–88
United States (US) Navy (USN) **5**, 12–13, 17–19, 21, 24, **34**, 36–37, **38**, **43**, 44, 46, 52–53, 57, 59, 61, **70**, 74–75, **80**, 83, **88**, 89–90
Unmanned Air Vehicle (UAV) 17, 29, 57, 61, 70, 82, **90**, 91–92
USS *Abraham Lincoln* 4, **5**, 12, 17, **53**, 64, 70
USS *Constellation* 12, 17, 42, **43**, 56, 59, 68, 83
USS *Kitty Hawk* 12, 17, 69, 83, **84**

Wadi Al Khirr **27**, **40**, 45–46, 49, **50**
Weapons of Mass Destruction (WMD) 5, 8–9, 32–33, 46, 70, 85
western desert 10, 14, 20, 26, 33, 37, **39**, **40**, **41**, 43, 46, 49, 59, 61, 63, 71, 81, 86